Favorite Ways to
Explore
Economics

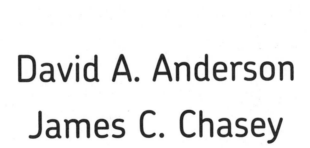

David A. Anderson
James C. Chasey

bfw
Worth

A Macmillan Higher Education Company

ISBN-13: 978-1-4641-4638-1
ISBN-10: 1-4641-4638-1

Printed in the United States of America

First Printing

Worth Publishers
41 Madison Avenue
New York, NY 10010
www.worthpublishers.com

CONTENTS

A Note to Students About Active Learning Experiments

Economics was the major of choice for rock stars like Mick Jagger and Young M.C., actors like Ben Stein and Cate Blanchett, big shots like Sandra Day-O'Connor and George H.W. Bush, and billionaires like Donald Trump. For some, however, the appeal of this exciting discipline is tempered by the challenge of grasping its fundamental concepts. We wanted to change that. The purpose of the active learning experiments in this book is to take you inside the box and show you how it feels to be an economic actor. That is, this book will lead you through activities that simulate production, sales, and various types of economic decision-making. Active learning has proven to be both popular and successful in eliciting the economic way of thinking. Your participation in experiments will make concepts easier to learn and remember. These activities will help to clarify economic concepts, but only if you are an attentive and engaged participant. Be sure to take part earnestly and behave honestly. Passive participants will not reap the same rewards as those who jump in and become involved. Please read the introduction and scenario for each activity before class. After each activity, reflect on the experiment overnight and bring the completed worksheet to the next class meeting.

While the practice problems and activities in this book will reinforce the fundamentals of economics as taught by any textbook, we have selected coverage that goes especially well with *Explorations in Economics*. In *Favorite Ways to Explore Economics* you will find practice problems that offer opportunities to polish skills taught in your textbook, and experiments that allow you to experience the dilemmas and incentives described in your textbook.

Above all, we hope that you enjoy this learning experience!

Best wishes,

Dave Anderson & Jim Chasey

About the Authors

David A. Anderson is the Paul G. Blazer Professor of Economics at Centre College. He received his Bachelor of Arts degree from the University of Michigan and his Masters and Doctoral degrees from Duke University. Prof. Anderson has published articles on active learning, classroom technology, and teacher evaluation, and on the economics of issues ranging from childbirth to the death penalty. He has received a National Endowment for the Humanities distinguished professorship, and grants for education projects from the 3M Foundation and the Andrew Mellon Foundation. Prof. Anderson speaks regularly on best practices for teaching economics to high school students. His other books include *Economics by Example, Economics in Modules, Krugman's Economics for AP*,* and *Explorations in Economics* (all available from Worth Publishers).

James C. Chasey received his Bachelor of Arts degree from Purdue University and his Master of Arts degree from the University of Illinois. As the Christa McAuliffe Fellow for Illinois, he received advanced training at the University of Chicago Graduate School of Business. Chasey has received the Freedoms Foundation Leavey Award, the Money Smart Award from the Federal Research Bank of Chicago, and the Purdue University outstanding education alumni award. He taught Advanced Placement Economics and general economics at Homewood-Flossmoor High School, and served as Adjunct Professor of Economics at the College of Dupage and at Governors State University.

Acknowledgments

The authors are grateful to the many who have contributed to this effort. Corey McCaffrey, Beth Stepanczuk, Cara Stepancauk, Nate Olsen, and Ashley Vinsel provided excellent assistance in preparing the manuscript. Hundreds of dedicated students field-tested the experiments and problem sets. Our families endured late hours and urgent deadlines. The faculty consultants at the AP Economics readings offered inspiration and support. Ann Heath, Enrico Bruno, and Dora Figueiredo at BFW/Worth Publishers provided tremendous support and encouragement. Most importantly, we thank the students who enthusiastically dive in and puzzle over the fascinating field of economics, and the instructors who give them the opportunity to achieve economic literacy.

Favorite Ways to Explore Economics

Chapter 1
AN INTRODUCTION TO THE ECONOMIC WAY OF THINKING

Classroom Experiment 1.A

Economics is All Around Us: Hot Dog Vendors on the Beach

Time Required*: 10 minutes*	***Materials****: none*	***Level of Difficulty****: low*

Purpose: *to demonstrate that economics is everywhere, and that optimal business strategies can be discovered with a small amount of economic reasoning.*

Textbook Coverage of Underlying Topics*: Explorations in Economics:* Chapter 1

INTRODUCTION

In the words of Nobel Laureate Paul Samuelson, economics can be "perfectly straightforward without being perfectly obvious." Optimal strategies aren't always obvious, but sometimes it's easier than you think to explain the behavior of business firms and make wiser decisions in your own endeavors with the help of a bit of economic reasoning. This experiment will put you into the shoes of an entrepreneur and ask you to make decisions about the three most important issues for new business owners: location, location, and location.

SCENARIO

The setting for this activity is a long beach with many hungry swimmers and sun worshipers. Imagine yourself as one of two hot dog vendors working this particular strip of beach. Whether or not you are one of the students asked to demonstrate your decisions on the simulated beach in your classroom, think carefully about where you would locate your hotdog stand under the circumstances described below. The scenario unfolds this way:

• The two hot dog stands on this beach have identical prices, products, and overall appeal.
• Beachgoers will purchase from whichever hot dog stand is *closest* to them.
• Beachgoers are evenly distributed along the beach.
• Only one hot dog vendor can move at a time.

In the classroom experiment, two representative hot dog vendors will be asked to station themselves on the beach, and then take turns changing their location (if desired) in response to the other's location. The goal for each is to maximize hot dog sales[1]. Note that the shoreline along which the vendors may locate is

---

[1] Assume that maximizing sales is the same as maximizing profits. This is true if the vendors can always sell another hot dog at a price that exceeds the cost of providing another hot dog. If the cost of selling another hot dog—the "marginal cost"—increases as more are sold, the vendors will only sell hot dogs as long as their additional revenue from selling one more exceeds the marginal cost.

a line from one side of the classroom to the other. There is no depth to the beach, meaning that they can move to the left or right along the beach, but they cannot venture forward into the dunes or backward into the water.

REFLECTIONS
(Please answer these questions *after* completing the classroom experiment.)

1. Describe the optimal strategy for choosing a location under the conditions described above.

2. In what situations do you see a similar strategy practiced near where you live?

3. What evidence of this strategy have you seen on a national scale?

 4. Can you think of applications of this strategy that go beyond retail sales?

AFTERTHOUGHTS

Believe it or not, you have just reasoned through some implications of spatial competition models described in the writings of economist Harold Hotelling. Although they are not immediately obvious, these findings and their retail applications make good sense after thought and experimentation. That is one of the reasons to study economics—there are important lessons about maximizing profit and happiness that elude the casual observer. The economic way of thinking can guide us to sensible solutions to everyday dilemmas; that's one of the things that makes economics valuable and exciting! We hope you agree.

Classroom Experiment 1.B

Production Possibilities Frontier Experiment: Links and Smiles

Time Required: *25 minutes*	***Materials***: *2 sheets of 8 1/2 x 11 paper* *1 roll tape* *1 pair scissors* *1 pencil or pen*	***Level of Difficulty:*** *low*

Purpose: *After deriving your own production possibility frontier, you will better understand (and remember) what it's all about and the reasons for its shape.*

Textbook Coverage of Underlying Topics: *Explorations in Economics:* Chapter 1

INTRODUCTION

A production possibilities frontier (also known as a production possibility curve) indicates all of the possible combinations of two goods that can be produced in one period using all available resources. By looking at a PPF, the trained eye can determine the opportunity cost of each of the goods at every level of production, and whether or not production occurs at an efficient level. This experiment allows participants to derive and demystify production possibilities frontiers. After experimenting with different production goals, you will gain an understanding of input specialization and increasing opportunity costs.

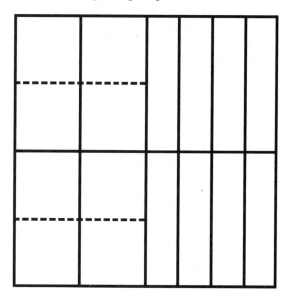

SETUP
There are two types of paper inputs used in this experiment: 5 1/2" x 1 1/16" strips, and 2 3/4" x 1 1/8" rectangles. To obtain enough of each paper input for the whole experiment, you will need two 8 1/2 x 11 sheets of paper. Stack the two sheets on top of each other and make the following folds:

1. Fold the two most-distant ends together.

2. Fold the new most-distant ends together.

3. Undo the last fold and fold each of the most-distant ends in so that they touch the center line.

4. Without doing any unfolding, fold *one* side in once more so that it touches the center line.

5. Unfold the papers and you should have creases where there are solid lines in the illustration above. Cut along the creases, and cut the four wider strips in half as indicated by the dotted lines. You should then have 16 strips and 16 rectangles.

SCENARIO

In this experiment every person represents a manufacturing firm. Firms will make links and smiles.

A *link* is a 5 1/2" x 1 1/16" strip of paper wrapped into a circle and taped in place. Subsequent links are put through the previous link and taped to interconnect the links, forming a paper chain, as are sometimes wrapped around Christmas trees.

A *smile* is manufactured by using scissors to round the four edges of a 2 3/4" x 1 1/8" rectangle and drawing two eyes and a smile on one side of the circle.

Although strips are best for making links, and rectangles are best for making smiles, creative cutting and taping will permit strips to be made into regulation smiles and rectangles to be made into regulation links. For example, a strip can be made into a rectangle by cutting it in half and taping the halves together, long edge to long edge.

Participants begin each round with 4 strips, 4 rectangles, a pen, a roll of tape, and a pair of scissors. Resources may not be carried over from one period to the next, and only one layer of paper may be cut at a time. Each round of production lasts 70 seconds. The production goals for each round are as follows:

Round 1: Make four smiles and as many links as you can.

Round 2: Make only links.

Round 3: Make only smiles.

Round 4: Make one smile and as many links as you can.

Record the number of links and smiles produced in each round.

	LINKS	SMILES
Round 1	_____	_____
Round 2	_____	_____
Round 3	_____	_____
Round 4	_____	_____

REFLECTIONS
(Please answer these questions *after* completing the classroom experiment.)

1. Draw your production possibilities frontier in the space below.

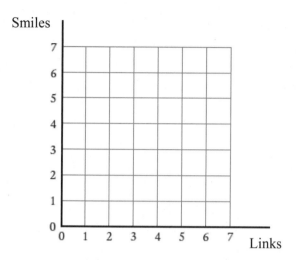

2. What was the opportunity cost of the first smile?

3. What was the opportunity cost of the last smile?

4. Why did the opportunity cost of making smiles increase as you made more of them?

5. In this experiment you used strips that were specialized for making links, and rectangles that were specialized for making smiles. Give two examples of real-world inputs that are specialized for the production of particular goods.

6. Explain how the use of specialized inputs results in a concave production possibilities frontier.

7. List two goods that are made from virtually identical (rather than specialized) inputs and illustrate the general shape of a production possibilities frontier for those two goods.

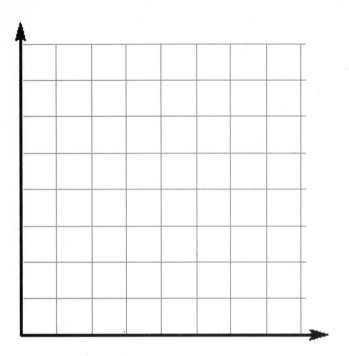

AFTERTHOUGHTS

Having acted as producers and derived production possibilities frontiers, you should come away with a better understanding of the implications of specialized resources and increasing opportunity costs. In subsequent classes you will be able to draw upon this experience to address issues of specialization and the role resources play in the shape of the PPF.

Favorite Ways to Explore Economics

Problem Set 1.1

Calculating Opportunity Cost

Workaholic Felix Alvarez is considering a trip to Sanibel Island, Florida for his spring vacation. He estimates that his roundtrip airfare would be $275.00, his car rental would cost $175.00, and his hotel expenses would be $950.00 for his one-week trip. By going on vacation, Felix would not be able to work and would therefore not earn his usual $1,250.00 per week. Felix spends the same amount on food wherever he is. He always eats in restaurants and his meals cost an average of $290.00 per week.

Calculate the "cost" of this vacation for Felix and explain why you did or did not include each of the components described above in your calculation.

Problem Set 1.2

Production Possibility Curves

Table 1 lists the various combinations of good X and good Y that can be produced in an economy. Use the information in Table 1 to answer questions 1–5.

1. Plot the following combinations of good X and good Y on Graph 1 and connect the points with a smooth curve.

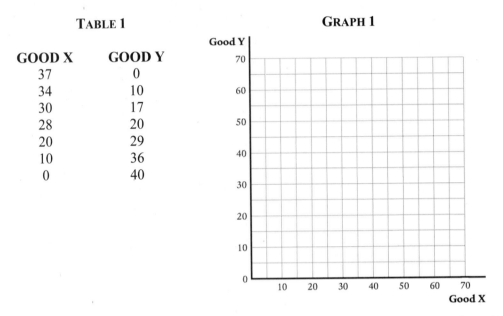

TABLE 1

GOOD X	GOOD Y
37	0
34	10
30	17
28	20
20	29
10	36
0	40

GRAPH 1

2. Calculate the cost of increasing good X production from 0 to 10 units in terms of the amount of good Y that could no longer be produced.

3. Calculate the cost of increasing good X production from 10 to 20 units in terms of the amount of good Y that could no longer be produced.

4. Calculate the cost of increasing good X production from 20 to 30 units in terms of the amount of good Y that could no longer be produced.

5. What happens to the opportunity cost of producing good X as more good X is produced?

Favorite Ways to Explore Economics

Suppose instead that Table 2 indicates the quantities that can be produced in the economy. Use the information in Table 2 to answer questions 6 through 10.

6. Plot the following combinations of good X and good Y on Graph 2 and connect the points.

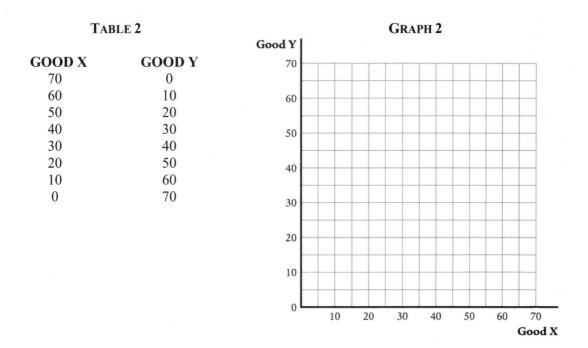

TABLE 2	
GOOD X	**GOOD Y**
70	0
60	10
50	20
40	30
30	40
20	50
10	60
0	70

7. Calculate the cost of increasing good X production from 0 to 10 units in terms of the amount of good Y that could no longer be produced.

8. Calculate the cost of increasing good X production from 10 to 20 units in terms of the amount of good Y that could no longer be produced.

9. Calculate the cost of increasing good X production from 20 to 30 units in terms of the amount of good Y that could no longer be produced.

10. What happens to the opportunity cost as the production of good X increases?

11. What characteristic of the inputs used to produce two goods leads to a production possibility curve with the general shape of Graph 1?

12. What characteristic of the inputs used to produce two goods leads to a production possibility curve with the general shape of Graph 2?

Problem Set 1.3

Shifting Production Possibility Curve

Using the given production possibility curve as a starting point, show the result of each of the following.

1. An increase in population.

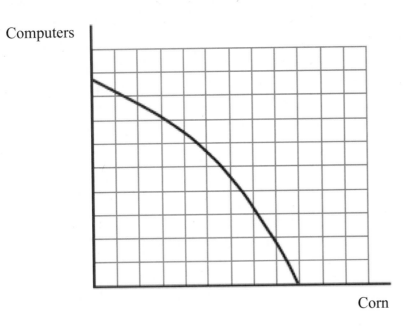

2. An improvement in technology applicable to corn production only.

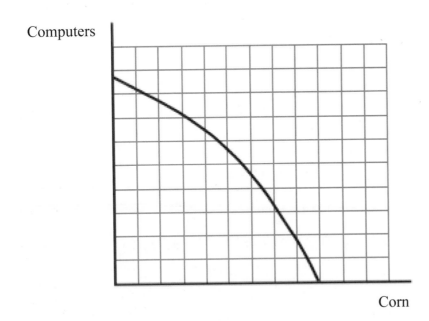

3. Increased literacy levels for all workers.

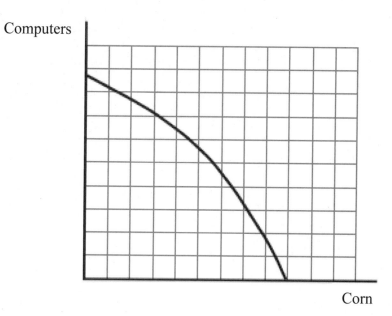

4. The depletion of non-renewable resources used in the production of both goods.

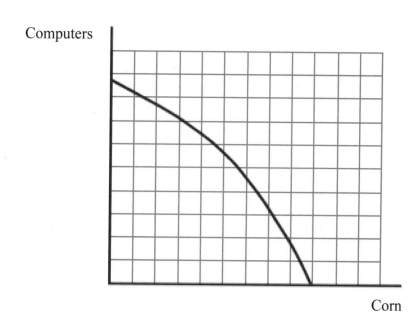

5. Increased consumer demand for computers.

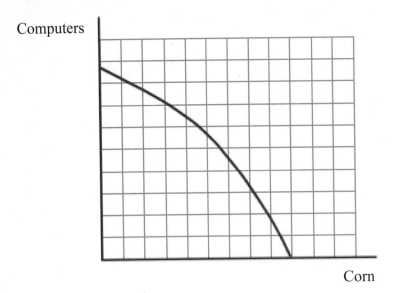

6. The development of a new production method that allows more computers to be made with any given amount of resources.

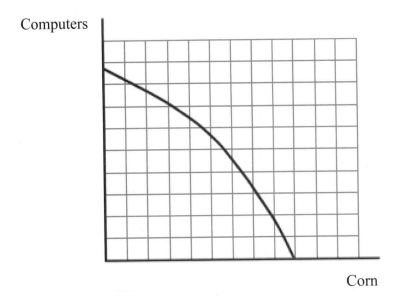

Problem Set 1.4

Three Economic Systems

1. What three types of economic systems can provide solutions to the central economic problem of scarcity (in addition to "mixed systems" which are combinations of the others)?

Indicate and explain which of the three types of systems would be best-suited for the following.

2. To achieve efficiency.

3. To have centralized decision making.

4. To organize production in a way that is easy to understand and reduces the possibility of job-related uncertainties.

5. To adjust rapidly to changing circumstances.

6. To organize production in a way that eliminates the need for centralized decision making and relies on the pursuit of self-interest.

7. Give an example of how the U.S. economy contains elements of each of the three types of systems.

Problem Set 1.5

The Economic Way of Thinking

Ada Okara has 9 hours available to study for her classes at Saint Aimee State University. The figures that follow are her best estimates of her scores on the upcoming exams in her classes.

HOURS OF STUDY	ECONOMICS	SPANISH	PSYCHOLOGY
0	20	30	35
1	39	51	53
2	56	65	69
3	71	77	79
4	82	86	87
5	86	91	92
6	88	95	95
7	89	97	97
8	90	98	98
9	91	99	99

Answer the following questions on the basis of the above information.

1. If Ada spends all of her time studying for Economics, what will her score be in Economics? Spanish? Psychology?

2. If Ada spends all of her time studying for Spanish, what will her score be in Spanish? Economics? Psychology?

3. If Ada spends all of her time studying for Psychology, what will her score be in Psychology? Spanish? Economics?

4. If Ada divides her time up evenly, studying 3 hours for each subject, what will her scores be in each of her classes?

5. Assume Ada Okara wants to maximize the total of her three exam scores. How would you recommend that Ada allocate her time? Why?

Chapter 2
SUPPLY, DEMAND, AND EFFICIENCY

Classroom Experiment 2.A

Buying and Selling Snipes in the Pit Market

Time Required*: 25 - 30 minutes*	***Materials****: recording sheets (provided below) and valuation cards*	***Level of Difficulty:*** *low to moderate*
Purpose: *To demonstrate the inner workings of a market and convergence to a market price.*	***Textbook Coverage of Underlying Topics****: Explorations in Economics:* Chapter 6	

INTRODUCTION

You have probably read in your textbook about how supply and demand curves are derived. In this exercise you will take part in the convergence of market forces that establishes quantities and prices to clear the market. This activity can be confusing to those who do not study the instructions, so please read the following carefully prior to the experiment.

SCENARIO

You will be assigned a role as either a buyer or a seller in what is called a *double-oral auction*. This name comes from the practice of buyers and sellers calling out their offers and demands such that all market participants can hear them. There are several versions of this experiment in the literature, some of which have no named product. Although the product you are buying or selling won't be tangible or change hands, we decided to name it a "snipe" to avoid the perplexing sale of nothing in particular.

Your instructor will give you a card indicating whether you are a buyer or a seller.

Buyers. If you are a buyer, the card you receive will also hold a number, which is the most you are willing to pay for a snipe. In other words, this is what a snipe is worth to you. If you can buy it for less than that amount, great. You have earned "consumer surplus"—a sort of bonus to buyers that equals the most they are willing to pay minus what they actually pay. You are not to pay more than the value on your card for a snipe. There is no reason to pay more for a snipe than what it is worth to you!

For example, if your card says $1000 and you manage to buy a snipe for $600, you get $1000 – $600 = $400 worth of consumer surplus. You would rather pay any price less than $1000 than not buy a snipe at all. You would be indifferent between paying $1000 and not buying a snipe (because you would be paying exactly what it is worth to you), and you would not be willing to pay $1001 or anything more than $1000 for a snipe. *Note: The prices used in these examples differ entirely from those used in the actual experiment in order to prevent price expectations based on these illustrations.*

Sellers. If you are a seller, the card will tell you the cost of "producing" a snipe. Snipes are raised to order, meaning that if you don't sell one, you don't need to raise one and you incur no costs. Thus, you will not sell a snipe for less than your cost of production. Your goal is to maximize your profit by selling a single snipe for as much above the production cost as possible. If you make a sale, your profit or "producer surplus" is calculated as the selling price minus your cost of production.

As an example, if your card indicates a production cost of $1000 and you manage to sell a snipe for $1500, your profit is $1500 − $1000 = $500. You would rather accept any price above $1000 than not sell a snipe at all. You are indifferent between selling for $1000 and not selling at all, because your profit at that price is zero. You would not be willing to sell your snipe for $999 or any other price below $1000.

The Workings of the Market. Your instructor will announce the beginning and ending of each trading period. You may only communicate with others about transactions during a trading period. When the period begins, buyers will shout out bids and sellers will shout out asking prices or "asks." Your voice is your only form of advertising in this market, so don't be timid. Remember that the amount on your card is your trading price at last resort—your intent is to transact at a price that is more favorable to you than the number on your card.

If you hear a price you would like to accept, or someone else accepts the price you are calling out, a transaction is born. As you are negotiating, take note of the prices from previous transactions that are posted on the chalkboard. They hold information about the spirit of the market. YOU MAY CARRY OUT AT MOST ONE TRANSACTION PER PERIOD. IF YOU MAKE A TRANSACTION BY BUYING OR SELLING A SNIPE, REPORT THE SELLING PRICE TO THE MARKET RECORD KEEPER (typically your instructor). AT THE END OF EACH MARKET PERIOD, WHETHER OR NOT YOU MAKE A TRANSACTION, RECORD THE RELEVANT INFORMATION ON YOUR SNIPE MARKET RECORDING SHEET. REMEMBER THAT EACH TRANSACTION PRICE MUST EXCEED OR EQUAL THE SELLER'S PRODUCTION COST AND FALL BELOW OR EQUAL THE BUYER'S VALUATION.

A Tax in the Snipe Market

(This is an optional variation on the above pit market experiment. The recording sheet, reflections, and afterthoughts below apply whether or not you have a round of taxes.)

SCENARIO

In the final period for the pit market game, a tax of $10 per snipe is imposed on the sellers of snipes. There is no tax on buyers. This means that while buyers will still pay up to the value on their card for a snipe, sellers cannot make a profit and therefore will not sell a snipe for less than $10 above their production cost. In a sense, taxes on sellers are part of the cost of bringing a product to market, so you can see this as increasing producers' costs by $10 per snipe. Thus, a seller with a card that reads $1000 will demand at least $1010 for the sale of a snipe. The other aspects of the market scenario are unchanged for this experiment with taxes.

Snipe Market Recording Sheet

PERIOD	ROLE (CIRCLE ONE)	YOUR VALUE/ COST	TRANSACTION PRICE	CONSUMER/ PRODUCER SURPLUS	AVERAGE MARKET PRICE
1	buyer / seller				
2	buyer / seller				
3	buyer / seller				
4	buyer / seller				
5 (with tax)	buyer / seller				

REFLECTIONS
(Please answer these questions *after* completing the classroom experiment.)

1. What happened to the average market price over the first four periods? That is, did it wander randomly or was there an observable trend?

2. Compare your surpluses from the first and fourth transactions. How would you explain the changes in your behavior and your surplus?

3. In what ways was this experiment similar to real-world markets?

4. On the basis of the information your instructor revealed after the exercise about consumers' and producers' values and costs, construct the market supply and demand curves for the snipe market.

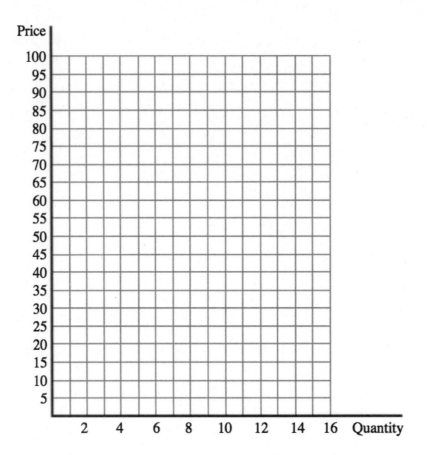

5. How did the average price in the final periods compare with the price that would maximize the sum of consumer surplus and producer surplus for all market participants—that is, the equilibrium price?

6. *(Answer the remaining questions only if you included a tax in the last period.)* How did the tax affect the average market price? Is that what you expected?

7. While the tax was imposed on the seller, did all of the burden fall on the sellers?

8. On the graph above, draw a new supply curve for sellers that reflects both the production cost and the tax cost. Does the new equilibrium price reflect what you observed in questions 6 and 7?

AFTERTHOUGHTS

Adam Smith said that in a free market with participants acting selfishly, the outcomes would be efficient, as if guided by an invisible hand. Hopefully you got a taste of this efficiency by observing that the pit market in your class converged to an outcome close to the equilibrium that maximizes consumer and producer surpluses. With a tax, the incidence is theoretically independent of the party paying the tax. That is, buyers and sellers share the tax burden in the same way whether the tax is on the buyers or the sellers. In this experiment, it is likely that you saw the $10 per snipe burden of the tax shared between the parties, in that the average price paid by buyers increased by less than $10, and the amount kept by the seller (the average price minus the tax) decreased by less than $10. The sum of the additional payment by buyers and the decreased amount kept by sellers is the amount of the tax. If the sellers bore the whole burden of the tax imposed on them, the price for buyers would not change and the amount kept by sellers would decrease by $10. This would only happen if the demand curve were horizontal. Can you draw a graph and figure out why this is true?

Classroom Experiment 2.B

Penning Supply and Demand Curves

Time Required: 15 minutes	*Materials*: Whatever pens or pencils you have on hand	*Level of Difficulty*: low to moderate. Players make decisions under uncertainty.
Purpose: to examine the influence of price on buying and selling decisions, and derive supply and demand curves along the way.	*Textbook Coverage of Underlying Topics*: *Explorations in Economics:* Chapter 6	

INTRODUCTION

Supply and demand curves are central to economic analysis, but far from intuitive upon first approach. We'd like to change that by having you reason through and form your own. In a way, you have supply and demand curves in your head for everything you could conceive of buying or selling. Of course, you may not have thought about them in the same way or with the same terminology that will be most useful in economics. Let's take a look at your present supply and demand "schedules"—a term used to describe either a table or a graph relating prices with quantities of a product supplied or demanded.

SCENARIO

When we refer to a "pen," let this mean a *working* (not broken) pen or mechanical pencil. (Wooden pencils are excluded.) You probably have a pen in your hand, a few in your backpack, and a few more in your dorm room or locker nearby. This activity will involve the actual buying and selling of pens, so think about what pens are worth to you. The first one is necessary to take notes with. A few more are nice as back-ups or to provide variety. Additional pens might have value in the future as you lose pens or wish to store them in several locations. Alternatively, if the price is right, you might want to sell pens. Perhaps you have an overabundance, you know where to get them cheaply, or you need some spare change. You might be willing to sell one or two spare pens for very little, and more if the price warrants foregoing pens that are more important to you or are harder to obtain. *Note that you can only sell pens and spend money that you have on hand, so bring some of each to class.* There will be only one round of this activity with one selling price, so you do not need to worry about conserving money or pens for additional rounds.

With the given scenario in mind, complete the table below. In the "I would buy" column, indicate the number of pens you would be willing to buy today in class with the money you have on hand at the prices listed. Be sure to write the total number for each price. For example, if you would buy 7 pens for 30 cents and 2 more if the price dropped to 20 cents, write "9" under "I would buy" at the 20 cents level. In the "I would sell" column, indicate the total number of pens you would be willing to sell at the different prices. *At each price you should have a zero either in the "buy" column or in the "sell" column,* because there is no sense in both buying and selling pens at the same price—that just makes for the effort of transactions with no gain. Leave the "market demand" and "market supply" columns empty for now.

PRICE (CENTS)	I WOULD BUY	I WOULD SELL	MARKET DEMAND	MARKET SUPPLY
140	_____	_____	_____	_____
130	_____	_____	_____	_____
120	_____	_____	_____	_____
110	_____	_____	_____	_____
100	_____	_____	_____	_____
90	_____	_____	_____	_____
80	_____	_____	_____	_____
70	_____	_____	_____	_____
60	_____	_____	_____	_____
50	_____	_____	_____	_____
40	_____	_____	_____	_____
30	_____	_____	_____	_____
20	_____	_____	_____	_____
10	_____	_____	_____	_____
0	_____	_____	_____	_____

In the diagram below, graph the numbers in your "buy" and "sell" columns.

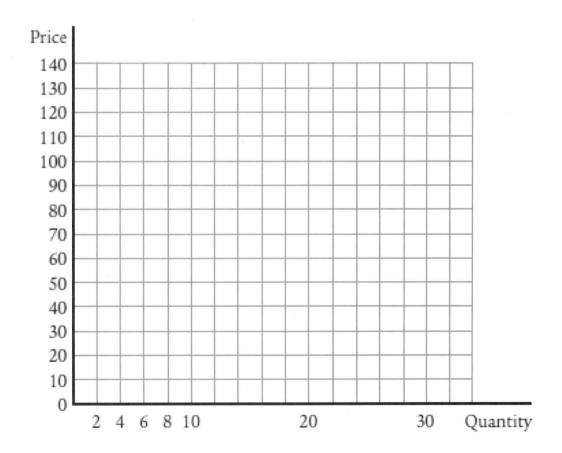

The graph of your "buy" quantities is your individual demand curve. The graph of the "sell" quantities is your individual supply curve. In class you will learn the quantities your classmates would buy and sell, and you can add up these quantities at each price to obtain the market demand and supply schedules.

REFLECTIONS
 (Please answer these questions *after* completing the classroom experiment.)

For items 2–5, be sure to use the numbers on your graphs to answer the questions.

The following observations will come in handy when answering the questions below: Note that the table you filled in above indicates the values to you of each incremental pen. That is, when the quantity you would buy increases after the price falls, that means that the pens you would buy at the lower price, but not at the higher price, are worth the lower price but not the higher price to you. For example, if you would buy 3 pens for 40 cents each and 5 pens for 30 cents each, that means that the 4th and 5th pens are each worth roughly 30 cents to you, and certainly less than 40 cents since you didn't want to buy them for 40 cents. (We have simplified the scenario here by considering 10 cent jumps in price. One cent increments would have permitted a more precise estimate of valuations.) Similarly, when the quantity you would sell increases as the price goes up, that means that for the pens you would supply at the higher price and not at the lower price, the minimum you could be paid to supply them is roughly the higher price. Thus, if you would supply 4 pens at 80 cents each and 5 pens at 90 cents each, the minimum you could be paid to supply the 5th pen is roughly 90 cents.

1. Draw a graph similar to the one above, but with a scale on the horizontal axis that accommodates the "market" demand and supply numbers for your class and graph them.

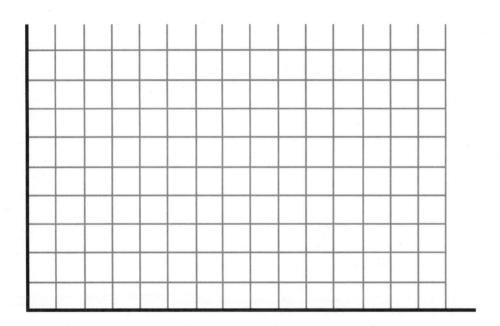

2. What is the first pen worth to you? _____ What is the first pen worth to the person in your class who values it the most? _____

3. How many pens would you purchase if the market price were 20 cents each? _____ What are those pens worth to you? (Add the value of the 1st + value of 2nd + ...) _____ The difference between what you would pay for them ($0.20 x quantity) and their total value to you is called "consumer surplus." What would your consumer surplus be if the price of pens were 20 cents each? _____

4. How many pens would you supply for 90 cents each? _____ What is the smallest amount of money that you could be paid to supply that many pens? (Add up the minimum you would accept for the 1st + the minimum for the 2nd + ...) _____ The difference between the actual amount you would be paid ($0.90 x quantity) and the smallest amount you would accept for that quantity is called the "producer surplus." What would your producer surplus be if the price per pen were $0.90? _____

5. On the graph below, draw a replica of your individual demand curve from above. Label it "D." Think about how this curve would be different if you just won $1000 in the lottery, or alternatively if, you decided to take notes using a laptop instead. (If you're not sure of the general changes in your demand curve, try filling out another table like the one above given the new scenarios.) Draw your demand curve with increased wealth and label it "D1." Draw your post-laptop demand curve and label it "D2."

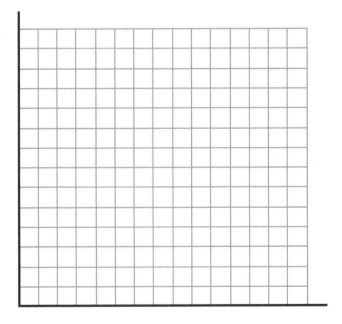

6. On the graph to the right, draw a replica of your individual supply curve from above. Label it "S." Think about how this curve would be different if you knew where to buy new ones for 10 cents each, or alternatively, if a 20-cent-per-pen-sold tax were imposed. Draw your supply curve with the 10-cent source and label it "S1." Draw your post-tax supply curve and label it "S2."

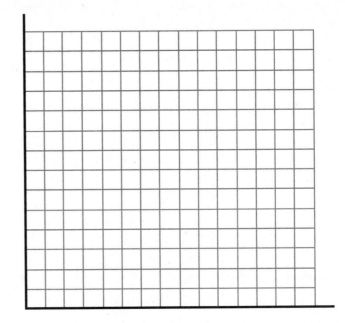

7. Beyond the changes described above,
a. What else would shift your demand curve to the right, meaning that you would buy more pens at any given price?

b. What else would shift your demand curve to the left, meaning that you would buy fewer pens at any given price?

c. What else would shift your supply curve to the right, meaning that you would supply more at any given price?

d. What else would shift your supply curve to the left, meaning that you would supply fewer at any given price?

AFTERTHOUGHTS

In some markets including the money market and the labor market, the same market participant can choose to be either a buyer or a seller, depending on where the price lies (the price of money being the interest rate and the price of labor being the wage rate). At low wage rates you might hire someone else to mow your lawn, while at high wage rates you might knock on doors offering to mow other people's lawns. If the interest rate were 1% you might decide to take out a loan to buy a car, whereas double-digit interest rates might bring you to put more money in the bank to be loaned out to others. In general, shifts in the market demand curve result from changes that affect people's willingness to pay for a good, such as advertising and income, and the number of consumers in the market. Shifts in the supply curve result from changes in the cost of producing the good or in the number of suppliers.

Favorite Ways to Explore Economics

Problem Set 2.1

Graphing Supply and Demand

The supply and demand schedules for Econ Videos in Econville are as follows:

PRICE PER ECON VIDEO	QUANTITY OF ECON VIDEOS DEMANDED	QUANTITY OF ECON VIDEOS SUPPLIED	SHORTAGE OR SURPLUS
$20.00	500	100	_____
$30.00	400	200	_____
$40.00	300	300	_____
$50.00	200	400	_____
$60.00	100	500	_____

1. Graph the demand for Econ Videos.

2. Graph the supply of Econ Videos in the graph to the right.

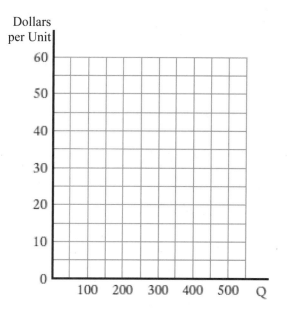

3. What is the equilibrium price of Econ Videos?

4. What is the equilibrium quantity of Econ Videos?

5. Fill in the Surplus or Shortage column.

6. What would result if the government of Econville set the price at $25.00?

7. What happens to price when a shortage exists in a market?

8. What happens to price when a surplus exists in a market?

9. What happens to price when an equilibrium exists in a market?

10. Do you think equilibrium or disequilibrium prices are most common in the "real world"? Why?

Problem Set 2.2

Shifting Demand Curves

On the graph provided, use a dotted line to illustrate the influence on demand (if any) of the stated change.

1. A new, less expensive substitute good is introduced into the market.

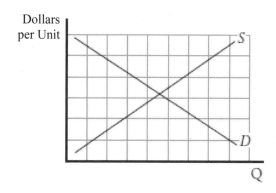

2. A law is passed that raises the age at which it is legal to consume this product.

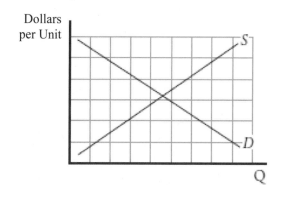

3. The price of a complementary good falls.

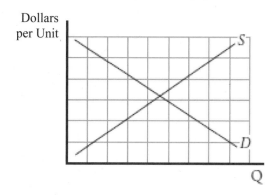

4. The government opens up its borders to completely free immigration.

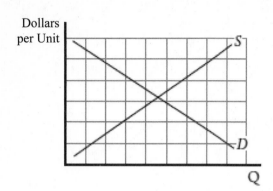

5. The good in question becomes more popular with consumers.

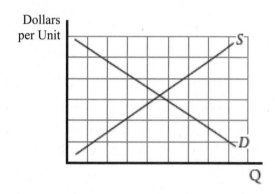

6. The cost of producing the good rises.

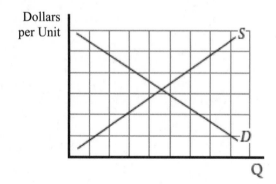

Favorite Ways to Explore Economics

7. There is an expectation of higher future prices. (What would happen to present demand?)

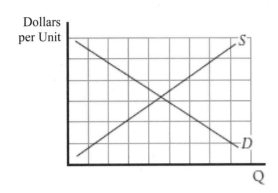

8. It is a normal good and buyers' incomes increase.

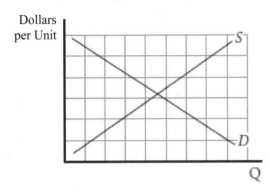

9. It is an inferior good and buyers' incomes rise.

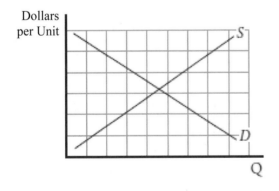

10. The price of the good rises.

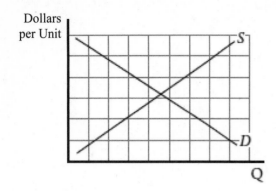

11. A change in technology makes production more efficient.

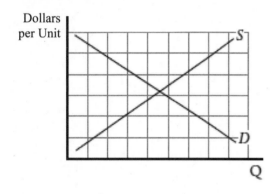

12. The price of a good that is neither a substitute nor a complement good rises.

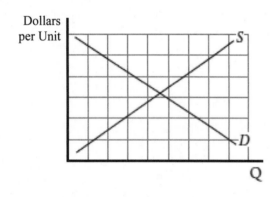

13. Create four problems like the ones above. Each should involve a change in a non-price determinant of demand that would shift the demand curve.

Problem Set 2.3

Shifting Supply Curves

On the graphs provided, use a dotted line to illustrate the influence on the supply curve (if any) of the given changes.

1. Advances in technology make production less expensive.

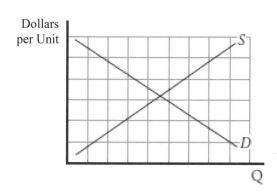

2. The resources formerly used to produce this product are banned.

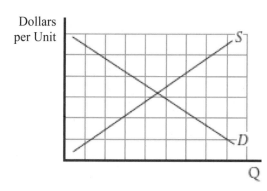

3. There is an increase in the selling price of another product that the same manufacturer can make instead of this product.

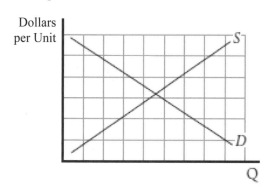

4. The selling price of this product increases.

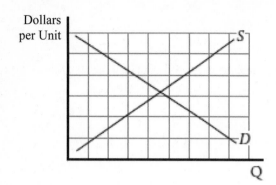

5. The good in question falls out of favor with consumers.

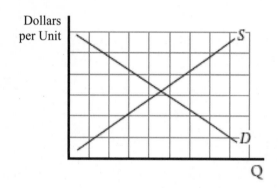

6. The cost of producing this product rises.

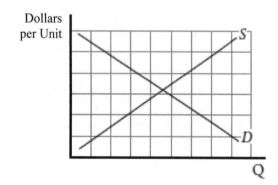

7. Producers expect higher future prices.

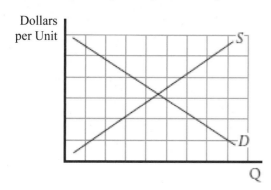

8. The government decides to subsidize the production of this good.

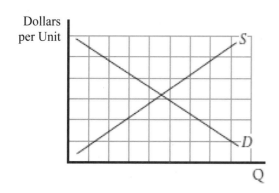

9. It is a normal good and buyers' incomes rise.

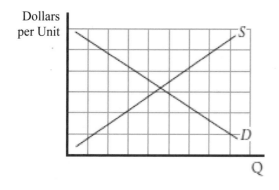

10. Foreign producers are now allowed to compete with domestic producers.

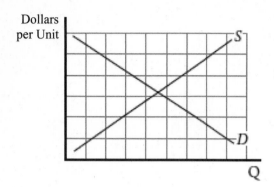

11. Create four problems like the ones above. Each should involve a change in a non-price determinant of supply that would shift the supply curve.

Problem Set 2.4

Shifting Supply and Demand

The supply and demand schedules for Ben Bernanke T-Shirts are given in the following table:

PRICE	QUANTITY SUPPLIED	QUANTITY DEMANDED
$15	150	10
13	130	30
11	110	50
9	90	70
7	70	90
5	50	110
3	30	130
1	10	150

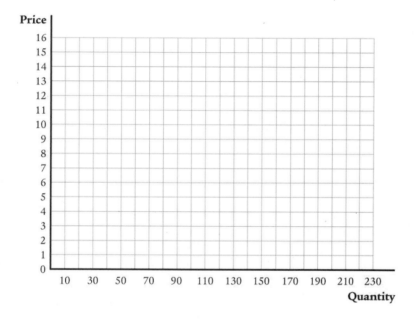

1. On the graph provided, plot the quantity demanded at each price. Draw a line to connect the plotted points and label the resulting demand curve "Demand 1."

2. Suppose a rise in the popularity of Ben Bernanke T-Shirts increases the quantity demanded at each price by 70. Plot the new demand curve and label it "Demand 2."

3. Now suppose a substitute for Ben Bernanke T-shirts, Alan Greenspan T-Shirts, is offered for sale in the market. Relative to Demand 2, the availability of substitutes reduces the quantity demanded of Ben Bernanke T-Shirts by 40 at each price. Plot the new demand curve and label it "Demand 3."

4. What will happen to the demand for Ben Bernanke T-Shirts as shown by Demand 3 if the price of Ben Bernanke T-Shirts increases from $9 to $11?

5. On the graph provided, plot the quantity supplied at each price. Draw a line to connect the plotted points and label the resulting supply curve "Supply 1."

6. Suppose that new technology makes these T-Shirts less expensive to produce. At each price the quantity supplied increases by 60. Plot the new supply curve and label it "Supply 2."

7. Now suppose that one of the firms producing Ben Bernanke T-Shirts goes out of business. Relative to Supply 2, this reduces the quantity supplied of Ben Bernanke T-Shirts by 30 at each price. Plot the new supply curve and label it "Supply 3."

8. What will happen to the supply of Ben Bernanke T-Shirts as shown by Supply 3 if the price of Ben Bernanke T-Shirts increases from $9 to $11?

Use the graph you have drawn to approximate the answers to questions 9 – 12 as closely as possible.

9. Identify the initial price and quantity of T-Shirts at the equilibrium of Supply 1 and Demand 1.

10. What is the new equilibrium price and quantity when demand shifts to Demand 2 if supply remains at Supply 1?

11. What is the new equilibrium price and quantity when supply shifts to Supply 2 if demand remains at Demand 2?

12. What is the new equilibrium price and quantity when demand shifts to Demand 3 and supply shifts to Supply 3?

Favorite Ways to Explore Economics

Problem Set 2.5

Elasticity

1. Calculate the total revenue at each price. Then use the Total Revenue Method (look at the change in total revenue as price changes) to categorize the price elasticity of demand as either elastic or inelastic in the range from the stated price to the price $10 higher.

PRICE	QUANTITY	TOTAL REVENUE	ELASTIC OR INELASTIC?
$100	1		—
90	2		
80	4		
70	7		
60	11		
50	15		
40	18		
30	20		
20	21		
10	21		

Problem Set 2.6

Stay in School Bumper Stickers

After Lucy Lugnut and her friend Diesel dropped out of school, they got into trouble with the law and ended up in prison. When they were released, they decided to capitalize on their newly developed skills in making license plates. They started a new business that made a metal version of bumper stickers that buyers could bolt to their bumpers or hang from their gun racks. It said, "STAY IN SCHOOL!
They studied the market and found that if they charged

$3.00 they would sell 6,250

$3.50 they would sell 6,125

$4.00 they would sell 6,000

$4.50 they would sell 5,500

$5.00 they would sell 4,500

$5.50 they would sell 3,000

Lucy and Diesel initially put their bumper sticker on the market for $3.50. They can produce any quantity of bumper stickers at a cost of $0.50 each and decided to hire you as a consultant to advise them about pricing.

1. Calculate the total revenue earned at each of the prices listed above.

2. Indicate whether demand is elastic or inelastic for each 50-cent price range between the prices listed above.

3. Would you advise them to raise the price to $4.00 even though they would sell fewer bumper stickers?

4. Would you advise them to lower the price to $3.00 in an effort to sell more?

5. Since Lucy and Diesel are the only providers of these bumper stickers, they can charge any price they choose. What price would you recommend? Why?

Problem Set 2.7

A Parking Lot Problem

WARNING: This problem set is not intended for the casual economics student. It contains material that may cause you to think! Be prepared to graph, analyze, calculate, and write short answers. User discretion is advised.

Once upon a time there was a school that let many students park in its lot when they drove to school. Then one day a big bad construction project was undertaken to add on to the school and most student parking was eliminated.

Near the school there was a church that decided to help the students out of this predicament (and themselves to a few bucks.) The church figured that if they charged

$50/month 1 student would park
$34/month 2 students would park
$28/month 3 students would park
$17/month 7 students would park
$10/month 11 students would park
$6/month 14 students would park
$2/month 19 students would park
$1/month 25 students would park

1. Plot this information about the demand for parking spaces on the graph to the right. Label your line D.

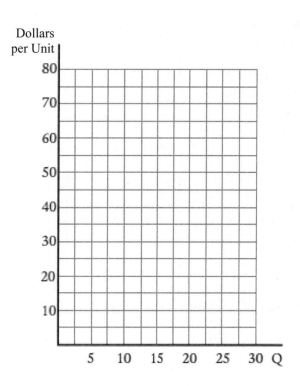

Now into our story comes the Wizard of Floz. In his infinite wisdom, he bans parking on all Village streets within a 1 mile radius of the school (an option that students had enjoyed before the ban). There is much rejoicing at the church and many hallelujahs are being said because now if they charged

$75/month 1 student would park
$58/month 3 students would park
$46/month 6 students would park
$36/month 10 students would park
$25/month 15 students would park
$18/month 20 students would park
$12/month 25 students would park
$10/month 29 students would park

2. Plot this information on your graph and label it D1.

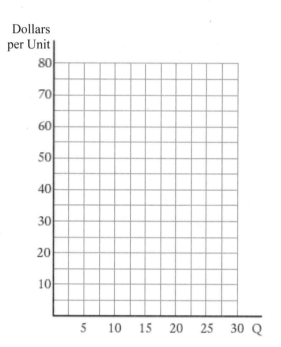

As the plot thickens, we further discover that the church has 15 available spaces each month.

3. Plot the unusual looking supply curve that results on your graph, and locate the equilibrium price.

4. Comment on the wisdom of a student petition to force the church to charge $10.00/month. What problem would arise? How could the church solve this problem without raising the price? Would you favor the proposed "price freeze" at $10/month? Why or why not?

5. To fill in the blanks that follow, calculate the total revenue for the church at each price and indicate whether demand is elastic or inelastic in the range between the prices.

If the church lowered the price from

$75 to $58 total revenue would go from _____ to _____ so demand is _____

$58 to $46 total revenue would go from _____ to _____ so demand is _____

$46 to $36 total revenue would go from _____ to _____ so demand is _____

$36 to $25 total revenue would go from _____ to _____ so demand is _____

$25 to $18 total revenue would go from _____ to _____ so demand is _____

$18 to $12 total revenue would go from _____ to _____ so demand is _____

$12 to $10 total revenue would go from _____ to _____ so demand is _____

6. Why shouldn't the church charge the highest possible price ($75)?

7. What is appealing to the church about charging the equilibrium price?

8. Why would the economics students (perhaps not all of them, but certainly all of the really intelligent, hardworking, cool-type economics students) like the church to charge the equilibrium price?

9. Who would not like the church to charge the equilibrium price?

10. What would be created if the price were set above the equilibrium price? (Use the term from economics.)

11. What would be created if the price were set below the equilibrium price? (Use the term from economics.)

Problem Set 2.8

Here is a Message for Us

SOUNDING BOARD

Editor's Note: The following letter was submitted by Ardmoreita R.C. Lang who is a member of the public information council of the American Association of Petroleum Geologists.

Dear Editor:

Many years ago there was a western type town called Wildcat, Wyoming. This was a very prosperous town and everyone had all they needed. A tribe of Indians lived on the outskirts of town who were buffalo hunters and they kept the town supplied with meat.

The town's people always had plenty of meat to eat although they did not have much in storage. The town also got meat from other buffalo hunters who brought in buffalo from far away lands.

This made it very hard on the local tribe, as they only received $2.00 per buffalo and with the imported meat there was not much demand for local hunts. The town's people did not care too much for the Indians anyway and didn't want them coming into their town.

The town also had a Government agency that was supposed to help the townspeople and the Indians. But it seemed the Agency was always against the Indians. Although some leaders in the Agency were good to the Indians, like "Buffalo Hansen," others, like "Trader Jackson," sought to destroy the local tribe.

Then it happened! The far-away buffalo hunters got mad at the town and would not deliver any more buffalo meat to them. Panic hit the town as there was very little meat in storage and everyone would be subject to rationing. The local tribe was at a loss, as they had no way to meet this sudden demand. The Indians were also were subject to rationing and had to wait in long lines and sometimes, after hours of waiting, found out they had run out of meat.

Most town people were not informed on what went on in this busy town and blamed the local Indian tribe for the shortage. (Some were so stupid they said the local tribe had purposely made unsuccessful hunts and had stampeded the buffalo over cliffs to create the shortage).

The Agency then came to the Indians and said, "We must have more Buffalo Per Day." (Now known as BPD.) "We must make our town independent, so we will not have to rely on far-away buffalo hunters anymore."

The Indians agreed. (As this was what they had tried to do all along.) But they had many problems. The bows and arrows were old and had been stacked in a teepee for years. They would have to be repaired or replaced. New ones were ordered, but the bow and arrow makers had two years worth of back orders. Inexperienced braves would have to be recruited as many of the older braves had left when the buffalo hunts were slow and wages were low—never to return. The buffalo also were not as plentiful as before and the hunters would have to travel longer distances, into deeper canyons, at more expense. The bows and arrows would cost more money and they would have to pay higher wages to the braves. The price of buffalo would have to be raised to $10.00 each to cover the expense of the hunt. Some of the townspeople cried, "Excessive Profits." The buffalo hunts were carried on at a fast pace. The Indians worked very hard.

Many moons before the crisis, the Agency had set it up so that the Tribe had to give them part of their buffalo earnings each year. But the Tribe returned from many, many hunts without even the smell of a buffalo. The Agency would then return a small amount of their earnings so they could invest it in other buffalo hunts. This was called a "Depletion Allowance." Most of this had already been taken away from the Tribe. This was another reason the Tribe had slowed investments in the hunts.

Although the Indians worked hard, the townspeople still complained. They said the hunters' horses messed up their land and smelled up the air, even though most of them had never been to the hunting grounds. They complained that the wagons that hauled the buffalo meat and the hunting gear should not be allowed on the main road, even though the Tribe paid the town for road permits and road use tax.

Some of the Indians started hunting from the water in canoes. This was a great expense to the Tribe but they felt this might increase the supply of buffalo. The townspeople cried that the Indians would ruin the rivers. Although the Tribe took every precaution, one buffalo did fall into the water. The Indian who had shot the buffalo cleaned up the mess by himself and paid all the expenses while the townspeople stood on the bank and complained. The Indian was required to take his canoe and leave town. All the buffalo that were taken from water hunting have been forgotten, but the "Buffalo Splash Story" is still talked about today.

The Agency formed a committee and sent them to the Indian village. They told the Tribe that this group would make their hunting safer. They would put saddles on the horses, tie the braves to them, put safety tips over arrow heads and give them hard-toed moccasins to wear. (All at the expense of the Indian Tribe.)

The Indians protested that this would greatly hamper the buffalo hunt and that the Tribe already had safety regulations. Why they even had their own safety council and safety braves checked every hunting party. But the Indians' argument fell on deaf ears and the new group stayed in command. The group was formed by townspeople consisting of store-keepers, bartenders, blacksmiths, and so on, none of whom had ever been near a buffalo hunt. The new group was called "Safety & Health for Indian Tribes."

Although the hunts became more and more expensive, it looked as if the Tribe might find enough buffalo for everyone to eat and maybe they could store some for the long, cold winters. Then an evil spirit came upon the Tribe. It was a leader from the Agency, good old "Trader Jackson." He said the depletion allowance should be taken away from the Tribe and the price should be rolled back to $2.00 per buffalo. The Agency and the townspeople agreed and it was done.

The beaten Indian Tribe put away their bows and arrows and returned to the reservation, never to hunt buffalo again. The winter was bad and all the townspeople starved to death. The town of Wildcat perished.

Don McElreath
Signal Oilfield Service, Inc.,
Casper, Wyoming

Answer the following questions based on the story.

1. On the graph below, show the effect of the "far away tribe" cutting off its supply of buffalo meat.

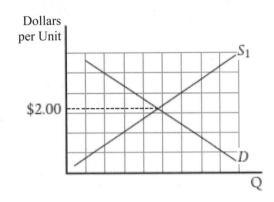

2. According to supply and demand analysis, what will happen to the price of buffalo meat when the far away tribe cuts off its supply?

3. If price were frozen at $2.00 per buffalo after the far away tribe cut off its supply, what would there be in the market for buffalo meat?

4. Show the effect of the Safety & Health for Indian Tribes act on the graph below.

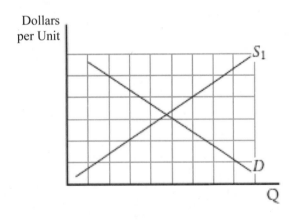

5. What tradeoffs must policymakers grapple with when deciding on safety regulations?

Problem Set 2.9

You Don't Have to be Old to be a Classic

Aging teen idol Ricky Rock decided to resurrect Woodstock. The only difference was that the event would be held in Illinois.

Headlining this psychedelic event would be Michelle Dinneen. Ricky and his sidekick Howard Spicer decided that if they held this event at the Galactic Music Theater in Pinley Tark and charged

$9.99 people would buy 32,000 tickets
$10.00 people would buy 28,000 tickets
$12.00 people would buy 23,000 tickets
$16.00 people would buy 19,000 tickets
$18.00 people would buy 17,000 tickets
$20.00 people would buy 15,000 tickets
$22.00 people would buy 13,000 tickets
$24.00 people would buy 11,000 tickets
$28.00 people would buy 7,000 tickets
$32.00 people would buy 5,000 tickets

1. Plot this information on the following graph.

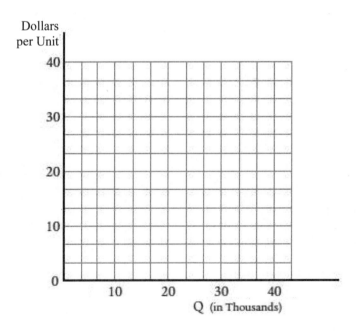

Rock music promoter and TV personality Tamra Syrett went to the Galactic Music Theater to calculate costs. She figured that if she could get

$10.00 per ticket she would offer 3,000 tickets for sale
$12.00 per ticket she would offer 6,500 tickets for sale
$14.00 per ticket she would offer 9,000 tickets for sale
$16.00 per ticket she would offer 11,000 tickets for sale
$20.00 per ticket she would offer 15,000 tickets for sale
$22.00 per ticket she would offer 17,000 tickets for sale
$24.00 per ticket she would offer 19,000 tickets for sale
$25.00 per ticket she would offer 20,500 tickets for sale
$30.00 per ticket she would offer 21,500 tickets for sale
$32.00 per ticket she would offer 22,000 tickets for sale
$36.00 per ticket she would offer 22,500 tickets for sale

2. Plot this information on the previous graph.

3. Identify the equilibrium price and quantity.

4. On the original graph, show what would happen if the "Ungrateful Alive" were added to the show and demand increased by 20%.

5. Demonstrate on the original graph what would happen if the traveling followers of the "Ungrateful Alive" (the Alive Feet) were rumored to be invading Pinley Tark to camp out and attend the concert. The local authorities would make Tamara Syrett pay those increased costs and she would therefore lower supply by 15%.

6. Identify on the original graph the new equilibrium price that would result from the combination of 4 and 5 above.

7. On the original graph, indicate a non-equilibrium price that would create a shortage.

8. On the original graph, indicate a non-equilibrium price that would create a surplus.

Problem Set 2.10

Price Floor

The following graph shows a market in which the government has imposed a price floor. Answer the following questions based on the graph.

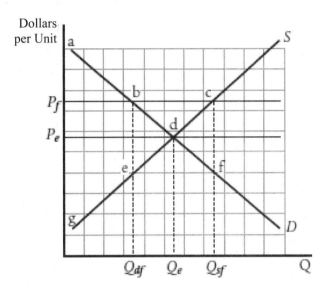

1. With this price floor in effect, what will happen to the actual price and quantity in the market and to the equilibrium (market clearing) price and quantity.

2. Comment on the efficiency of the equilibrium price and quantity that would prevail without the price floor in effect.

3. With the price floor in effect, what quantity would consumers want to purchase?

4. With the price floor in effect, what quantity would producers be willing to supply to the market?

5. With a price floor of Pf, what quantity would change hands and at what price?

6. What is the result of the quantity supplied being larger than the quantity demanded?

Problem Set 2.11

Price Ceiling

The following graph shows a market in which the government has imposed a price ceiling. Answer the following questions based on the graph.

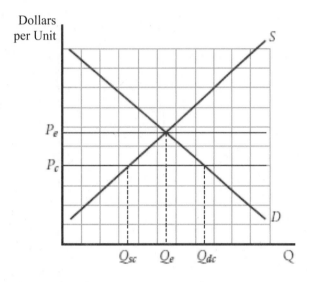

1. Interpret the effect of this price ceiling on the equilibrium (market clearing) price and quantity, and on the actual price and quantity in the market.

2. Comment on the efficiency of the equilibrium price and quantity that would prevail without the price ceiling in effect.

3. With the price ceiling in effect, what quantity would consumers want to purchase?

4. With the price ceiling in effect, what quantity would producers be willing to supply to the market?

5. With a price ceiling of Pc, what quantity would change hands and at what price?

Problem Set 2.12

Budget Lines

1. Suppose that a consumer has an income of $10 per period, and that he must spend it all on meat or potatoes. If meat is $1.00 per pound and potatoes are $.10 per pound, draw the consumer's budget line on the graph.

2. In the previous case, what would happen to the consumer's budget line if his income increased to $12 per period?

3. What would happen to the budget line in problem 2 if the price of meat increased to $2.00 per pound?

4. What would happen to the budget line in problem 3 if the price of potatoes increased to $.20 per pound?

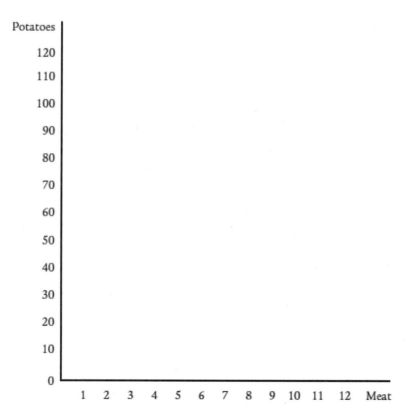

Chapter 3
PRODUCTION COSTS AND PERFECT COMPETITION

Classroom Experiment 3.A

Diminishing Marginal Product Experiment: The Econville Link Factory

Time Required: 20- 30 minutes	*Materials*: Stack of 81/2" X 11" paper (can have been used previously—recycle!) Two or three tape dispensers with tape Two or three pairs of scissors Two or three student desks	*Level of Difficulty:* low to moderate
Purpose: to demonstrate the reality of diminishing marginal product and provide data with which to calculate cost curves.	*Textbook Coverage of Underlying Topics*: *Explorations in Economics:* Chapter 5	

INTRODUCTION

When a car gets stuck in the snow, or someone gets hurt in an accident, or there's a new train set to be put together, the first few people who come to provide assistance do a lot of good. As more people join the effort and try to help out, their contributions become less and less valuable. When Uncle Charlie enters the room as the 10th person trying to put the train track together, he's more disruptive than helpful. There's a lesson to be learned here about manufacturing. As you might have anticipated, you're about to experience it first hand.

SCENARIO

In this experiment two or three factories within the classroom will produce *links*. You may remember this product from the *links and smiles* experiment. A link is a strip of paper approximately 51/2" x 11/4" cut from an 81/2" x 11" sheet. The strip is then wrapped into a circle and taped to form a ring. The next strip is cut, placed *through the previously made ring,* and taped to interconnect the two paper rings to form the beginnings of a "paper chain." The process is repeated for as many links as you can produce within the given time.

Production in the link factories proceeds as follows:

1. Each of the 2–3 factories gets one desk to work with. Your instructor will set these desks up in the front of the room with one stack of paper (ten sheets is enough), one pair of scissors, and one tape dispenser on each desk.
2. Each factory begins with a single production worker.
3. Production periods last 45 seconds, beginning and ending with a signal from your foreman/instructor.
4. After each production period, the employees at each plant count the number of *completed and linked* links made and report this number to the foreman for record keeping on the board. The foreman reserves the right to inspect each of the chains to assure quality control.
5. Before starting each successive production period, all bits of tape, paper strips, and partially made links are discarded, and one additional worker (but no more tape dispensers, scissors, or desks) is added to each factory. *Note that the workers are the variable input in this production process, and the scissors, tape, paper, and desk are the fixed inputs.*

Steps 3 through 5 will be repeated for a total of five or more production periods, with one new worker added to each factory each period.

Record the total output produced with each number of workers for use in the reflections below.

REFLECTIONS
(Please complete this section *after* completing the experiment above)

Your factories may or may not have produced results that would be considered typical. The following figures show what might happen in a typical links factory.

1 worker produced 2 links
2 workers produced 6 links
3 workers produced 8 links
4 workers produced 9 links
5 workers produced 9 links

1. Complete the following table based on production in your plant. If you did not work in a plant, you may base your answers on the figures provided above.

WORKERS (INPUTS)	TOTAL PRODUCT	MARGINAL PRODUCT
1		
2		
3		
4		
5		

2. Plot the data from your table in the graphs below and connect the dots to create the total product curve and the marginal product curve.

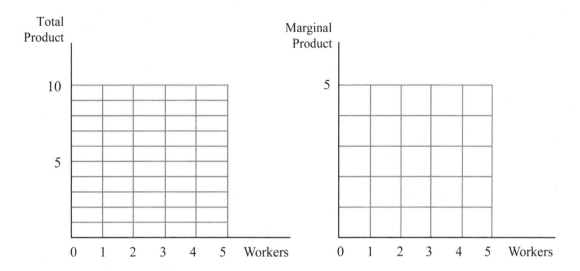

3. Can you identify any relationship between the graphs of marginal product of labor and total product of labor?

4. Look up the definition of diminishing marginal returns in your text. Substitute the links factory terminology for the economics jargon and re-write the definition. At what point in the typical links factory did diminishing returns set in? _____

5. What do you think would happen to marginal product if we continued to add additional workers? Do you think total product could ever fall? If so, what would have to be true about marginal product to make total product fall?

6. On the graphs for question 2 above, extend the total product and marginal product curves with dotted lines to show what a declining total product curve would look like, and what the marginal product curve would look like if total product did actually decline.

7. Now let us assign numbers to some of your costs. Rent for the desk was $10.00 per period, interest on the loan used to purchase the scissors was $5.00 per period, and labor costs were $10.00 per worker per period. Calculate the missing values in the table below using the data from the typical links factory (not your own) provided above. Treat labor as your only variable input (for simplicity we are disregarding paper costs).

OUTPUT	TOTAL FIXED COST	TOTAL VARIABLE COST	TOTAL COST
0	_____	_____	_____
2	_____	_____	_____
6	_____	_____	_____
8	_____	_____	_____
9	_____	_____	_____

8. Plot the figures from your table on the graph below.

Notice that we could derive the total variable cost graph from the total product graph by flipping the axes (placing labor on the vertical and output on the horizontal axis) and multiplying each quantity of labor by the wage to obtain the total variable cost.

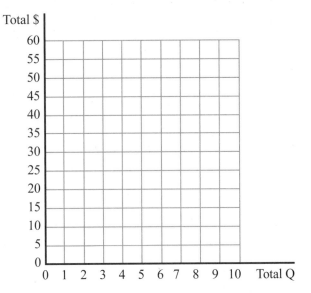

9. How are the total cost, variable cost, and fixed cost curves related to each other?

10. Suppose that links sell for $7.00 each. How would you determine the total revenue gained from selling links?

11. How would you determine profit or loss from selling links?

12. Complete the following table. You may obtain the total cost figures from the table for question 7 above.

Q	TOTAL COST	TOTAL REVENUE	PROFIT/LOSS
0	_____	_____	_____
2	_____	_____	_____
6	_____	_____	_____
8	_____	_____	_____
9	_____	_____	_____

13. If you could produce any of the quantities in this table, what amount would you choose? _____. Why would you not be willing to produce nine and take in more money?

14. Add the total revenue curve to your graph for question 8.

15. What does the vertical distance between total revenue and total cost represent?

AFTERTHOUGHTS

Whew! If you made it this far you've put in a lot of good work. You have now generated your own economic data and used it to derive many of the important relationships in microeconomics. If you ever have questions or concerns about firm behavior, look back at this experiment and remind yourself where those curves come from and why the slopes and intersections are important. Good work!

Classroom Experiment 3.B

Learning Graphs the Fun Way: Blind Curve

Time Required: *25 minutes*	**Materials**: *one sheet of paper per person and one file folder per two people*	**Level of Difficulty:** *low to moderate.*
Purpose: *to help students familiarize themselves with complex graphs.*	**Textbook Coverage of Underlying Topics**: *Explorations in Economics:* Chapter 5	

INTRODUCTION

Learning to draw graphs correctly is perhaps the most important skill learned in some economics courses. It can also be the most difficult. This exercise will allow you to practice drawing graphs and think carefully about the relationships between the lines on the graphs. After concentrating on the intersection points and shapes as you will here, you should have an easier time remembering the accurate relationships and the critical junctures when you go to apply the graphs to answer worthwhile questions.

SCENARIO

Your instructor will divide the class into pairs. You and your partner can then arrange your chairs so that one of you faces the chalkboard and the other faces the back of the room. Your desks should touch each other in the middle. (If you have tables rather than desks with chairs attached, arrange your chairs on either side of the same table.) Place the file folder in between the two of you so that you cannot see the paper on your partner's side of the table/desk. Your instructor will draw a graph on the board, allowing only those facing the board to see it. The objective of the exercise is for the participants who are facing the board to describe the graphs to their partners so that the partners can draw them. Those facing the chalkboard are not to look at the graphs their partners are drawing, and those drawing the graphs are not to look at the chalkboard.

In the event that you are already familiar with the name of the lines on the graph, you are not allowed to convey or inquire about any names. The student who is describing the graph must proceed with phrases like, "The first line starts near the top of the vertical axis. It is a straight line with a slope of about negative one. A second line, with a slope of about positive one, starts just above the origin on the vertical axis and crosses the first line in the middle. A third line starts where the first line started and bisects the distance between the vertical axis and the first line...." Be clear and creative in your explanations. When you think you have completed your artwork, take a look and see how you did. Then switch seats and get ready to do it again with the roles reversed.

REFLECTIONS
(Please answer these questions *after* completing the classroom experiment.)

1. How did you do? Was your diagram close to being correct?

2. What is the name of the graph you drew?

3. What is important about the location of the intersection of the lines you drew? (You may look up the graph in your book or notes to learn the answer to this.)

4. What is significant about the slope of the lines you drew? (Ditto)

AFTERTHOUGHTS

This activity provides a memorable introduction to valuable diagrams. As a positive externality, it is also an excellent exercise in giving instructions. We hope it will help you learn the subtleties of economic models and the pitfalls of common communication.

Problem Set 3.1

The Fixed, Variable, and Total Cost of Production

The table below provides production cost data for a firm.

OUTPUT	VARIABLE COST	FIXED COST	TOTAL COST
0	_____	_____	100
1	100	_____	_____
2	175	_____	_____
3	225	_____	_____
4	250	_____	_____
5	260	_____	_____
6	275	_____	_____
7	325	_____	_____
8	400	_____	_____
9	500	_____	_____
10	700	_____	_____

1. Fill in the blanks in the table.

2. Graph variable cost, fixed cost, and total cost on the graph to the right.

3. When graphed, what is the relationship (if any) between variable cost and total cost? Why?

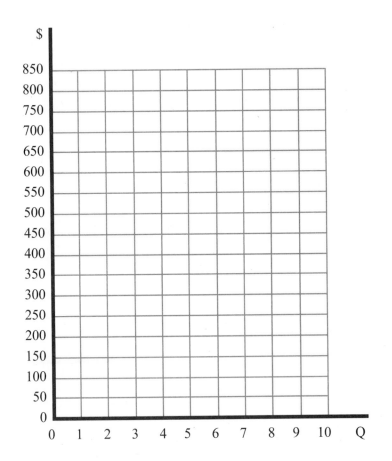

Problem Set 3.2

Daphne's Apparel Shop

Classify the following as Fixed Costs or Variable Costs for Daphne's Apparel Shop, a clothing manufacturer:

COSTS	FIXED COSTS	VARIABLE COSTS
1. Rent	_____	_____
2. Thread	_____	_____
3. Buttons	_____	_____
4. Wages	_____	_____
5. Electricity	_____	_____
6. Cloth	_____	_____
7. Equipment Rent	_____	_____
8. Shipping Costs	_____	_____
9. Insurance	_____	_____
10. Property Taxes	_____	_____

Calculate the following costs for Daphne's Apparel Shop.

PRODUCTION	FIXED COST	VARIABLE COST	TOTAL COST
0	_____	_____	5
1	_____	6	_____
2	_____	9	_____
3	_____	13	_____
4	_____	18	_____
5	_____	25	_____
6	_____	34	_____
7	_____	49	_____
8	_____	68	_____

Graph variable cost, fixed cost and total cost for Daphne's Apparel Shop on the following graph.

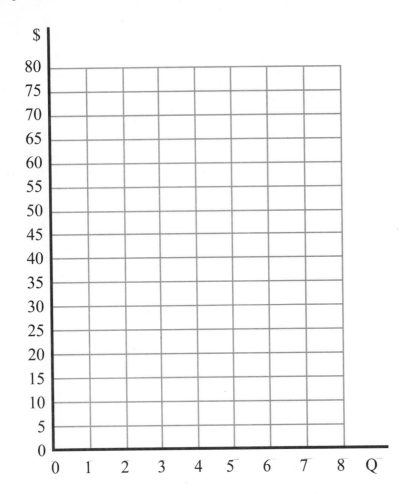

Problem Set 3.3

Cost Curves – The Un-University

Consider the following hypothetical situation. You are in the business of running a fake university. It is a true party school where there are no classes, no exams, no assignments, just dorms and classroom buildings. Students who can't make it anywhere else come to your university to perk up and get a chance to feel successful again. People over 30 believe you run a legitimate school. Tuition to your school is $30 per month. However, your costs are high. You must pay $50 per month in illegal bribes to the head of the State Board of Certification to maintain your accreditation. Without the bribes you could not operate at all. You must pay your professors according to the number of "Un-students" they have enrolled. Any student who enrolls in classes but does not attend is an "Un-student." The following table lists the total payment to professors depending on enrollment.

PROFESSOR'S MONTHLY FEE	NUMBER OF "UN-STUDENTS" ENROLLED
$50	1
$60	2
$70	3
$80	4
$85	5
$87	6
$90	7
$95	8
$100	9
$105	10
$110	11
$115	12

1. Graph total cost, fixed cost, variable cost, and total revenue on the graph below.

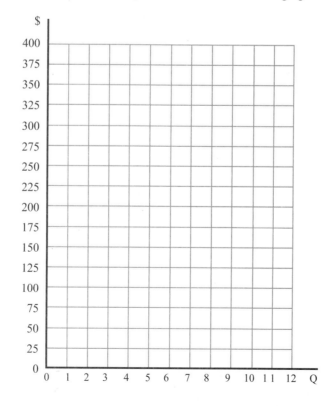

2. How many "Un-students" must you have to break even (rounded down to the nearest whole "Un-student")?

3. What is the smallest number of "Un-students" you would accept and still remain open in the short run (for any one year), rounded down to the nearest whole "Un-student"?

4. What would your answer to Question 3 be if the bribe to the Certification Board were to change to $100 per month?

Chapter 4
IMPERFECT COMPETITION
....

Classroom Experiment 4.A

A Cartel Growing Bananas

Time Required: 5 - 10 minutes	**Materials**: *scrap paper to use as production-report sheets*	**Level of Difficulty:** *low to moderate*
Purpose: *to demonstrate the temptation to cheat within a cartel.*	**Textbook Coverage of Underlying Topics**: *Explorations in Economics*: Chapter 8	

INTRODUCTION

Oligopoly firms sometimes face the temptation of colluding together, legally or illegally, and act like a monopoly. If successful, this would allow them to earn the same level of profits that a monopoly would, and these profits could be divided among the firms in a mutually beneficial manner. A group of firms working together in this way is called a cartel. OPEC, the Organization of Petroleum Exporting Countries, exemplifies both the intent and the pitfalls of cartels. Before you read more about this market structure, it will be informative to wear a cartel member's shoes for a while.

SCENARIO

You will soon meet in Geneva with fellow members of the Bananas Independently Grown (BIG) cartel. The president of your cartel, your instructor, has a proposal for you to consider that s/he states will allow your cartel to gain more profits to be divided among the members. After listening to the proposal, you will be asked to report your production level for the subsequent period as a percentage of your usual production level. For example, if you will produce half of your usual amount, write down 50%. If you will produce the same amount as before, write down 100%, and so on. In addition to the options presented by your cartel president, you should also be aware of incentives to cheat. That is, at least in the short run, you can produce additional bananas beyond the proposed limit and ship them off in the dark of night at a price close to the cartel price. This will earn you some extra cash, but if many of the cartel members do this, too many bananas will be supplied and the intended monopoly-level price and the corresponding profits will fall for everyone. Listen to your president's ideas and then write down the actual percentage of your usual banana crop that you will produce next period. Your production report will be completely anonymous.

REFLECTIONS
(Please answer these questions *after* completing the classroom experiment.)

1. Describe the outcome of your cartel experiment.

2. What was your production level and what motivated you to produce that amount?

3. Who benefits and who is harmed by greed among members of a cartel?

4. Who benefits and who is harmed by profit maximization by a monopoly?

5. Do you have any ideas for how to handle the problem of greed when it is destructive?

AFTERTHOUGHTS

Indeed, cartels like OPEC are seldom able to restrict the quantity produced to the mutually beneficial levels. They typically end up producing too much (from the sellers' standpoint) and earning less than planned. The difficulty of monitoring the output of member nations can cause insurmountable temptation, as greed is all too often the overarching motivator. Fortunately for consumers, cartel failure results in lower prices and higher quantities than if the ventures were to succeed.

Classroom Experiment 4.B

A Monopoly Making Dough

Time Required: *15-20 minutes (less if the table is filled in before class)*	***Materials***: *none*	***Level of Difficulty***: *moderate*
Purpose: *to provide insight into the forces of market structure, including the influence of monopoly on price and quantity.*	***Textbook Coverage of Underlying Topics***: *Explorations in Economics:* Chapter 8	

INTRODUCTION

Perhaps you've been in an airport where a single pizza purveyor represents the only choice for those in the mood for food. And then there are the business districts brimming with pizza shops where you can buy a whole pie for about the price of a slice in the airport. What's the deal with that? Is it natural? Is it good economics? Let's find out!

SCENARIO

Phase I – The Monopoly

You make pizza like no other. Your product is inches thick, dripping with cheese, and bursting with flavor from a secret ingredient Colonel Sanders would have given his right wing for. Your exclusive human capital—talents and secrets—give you a monopoly on the gourmet pizza business in your area, and you face the entire market demand for gourmet pizza as illustrated in the graph below. Be sure to read the graph correctly. It indicates that you can sell one pizza for $10, or two for $9 each, or three for $8 each, and so on.

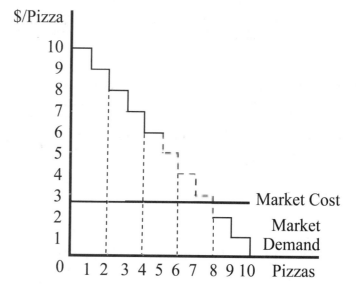

Each pizza costs $2.50 to make. What price and corresponding quantity should you choose to maximize profits? In order to find out, fill in the following table and add the marginal revenue and marginal cost curves to the diagram above:

PIZZAS	TOTAL REVENUE	MARGINAL REVENUE	TOTAL COST	MARGINAL COST	PROFIT
1					
2					
3					
4					
5					
6					
7					
8					
9					
10					

Remember:

> **Total revenue** is price times quantity.
> **Marginal revenue** is the total revenue from a given quantity minus the total revenue when selling one pizza fewer.
> **Total cost** is the sum of all costs associated with making a given quantity.
> **Marginal cost** is the total cost of a given quantity minus the total cost when making one pizza fewer.

What is your optimal price? _____ How many will you sell at that price? _____

Phase II – Competitors Enter

Few secrets elude the information age, and alas, a disgruntled worker at your pizzeria has shared your baking secrets on the Internet. Everyone in the class is now a potential entrant into the gourmet pizza market. Everyone's marginal cost is $2.50. As always, this includes the opportunity cost of your time. Thus, if you can get at least $2.50 per pizza, there's nothing else you could do with your time to earn more money.

Your instructor represents the consumers in the market. All existing pizza makers are assumed to make pizza of identical quality, and the consumers will purchase from whoever has the lowest price. As your instructor inquires about available prices, you have the option to enter the pizza market or not depending on the going price. When more than one pizzeria is operating, the consumer demand is divided evenly among the existing pizzerias.

REFLECTIONS

1. You have studied firm behavior in your textbook. When you chose your profit-maximizing price and quantity as a monopolist, did your behavior correspond with the rules for profit maximization explained in your textbook? Explain.

2. Describe the result of entry into the gourmet pizza market—what changed?

3. Do your findings agree with economic theory in terms of the price in a competitive market and the influence of competition on quantity?

4. Who benefits and who loses due to the introduction of competition?

5. Some say the best pizza comes from Chicago or New York, and not from the monopolist at the airport. Could market structure have something to do with this as well? Explain.

6. As an entrepreneur working on innovative recipes (or pharmaceuticals or whatever), how are one's incentives improved by the ability to operate a monopoly?

7. What solutions or compromises would you suggest to resolve this dilemma between the costs and benefits of market power?

AFTERTHOUGHTS

This experiment highlights the influence of market power. Your findings help to explain both the corporate battles for patents, mergers and acquisitions, and the enactment of antitrust legislation to prevent excessive market power. For example For example, Universal Music Group acquired EMI Recorded Sound in 2012, while the U.S. government took up a case against AT&T's proposed takeover of T-Mobile in 2011. Antitrust policy and enforcement decisions are common and important, which is why it's wise for you to have insight into the importance and dynamics of market power.

Problem Set 4.1

Daphne's Apparel Shop as a Monopoly

Complete the table below.

Q	P	TR	MR	FC	VC	TC	PROFIT
0	13	—		5	—	—	—
1	12	—	—	—	6	—	—
2	11	—	—	—	9	—	—
3	10	—	—	—	13	—	—
4	9	—	—	—	18	—	—
5	8	—	—	—	25	—	—
6	7	—	—	—	34	—	—
7	6	—	—	—	49	—	—
8	5	—	—	—	68	—	—

1. Fill in the blanks in the table.

2. Determine the profit-maximizing output and price for this monopolist.

3. Graph demand and marginal revenue.

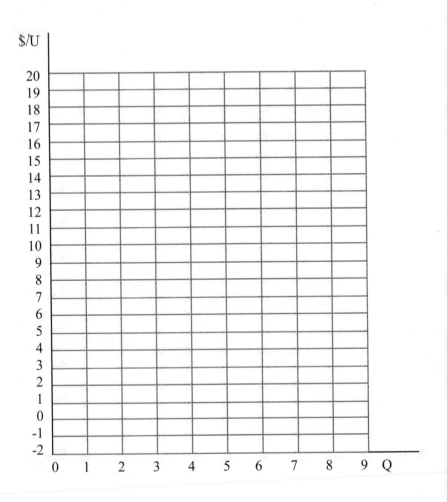

Problem Set 4.2

Total Revenue, Marginal Revenue, and Average Revenue

Assume that the following figures are for a monopolist who has just introduced a patented product. Market research shows the following:

PRICE	QUANTITY	TOTAL REVENUE	MARGINAL REVENUE
$11	0	_____	_____
$10	1	_____	_____
$9	2	_____	_____
$8	3	_____	_____
$7	4	_____	_____
$6	5	_____	_____
$5	6	_____	_____
$4	7	_____	_____
$3	8	_____	_____
$2	9	_____	_____
$1	10	_____	_____

1. Calculate and fill in the blanks for total revenue.

2. Calculate and fill in the blanks for marginal revenue.

3. Graph the demand curve.

4. Graph marginal revenue.

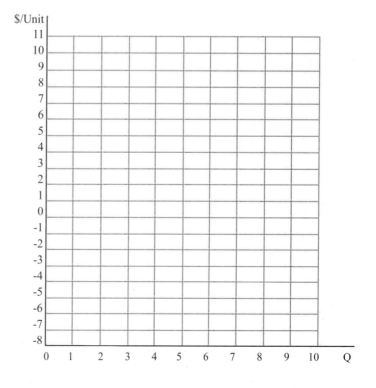

Problem Set 4.3

Marginal Revenue and Elasticity

To answer the following questions use the figures for total revenue and marginal revenue from Problem Set 4.2, "Total Revenue, Marginal Revenue, and Average Revenue."

1. Fill in the blanks with the appropriate total revenue and price elasticity figures.

    A. At a price of $1 total revenue is _____\
       At a price of $2 total revenue is _____\
       Therefore in this price range the demand curve is _____

    B. At a price of $2 total revenue is _____\
       At a price of $3 total revenue is _____\
       Therefore in this price range the demand curve is _____

    C. At a price of $3 total revenue is _____\
       At a price of $4 total revenue is _____\
       Therefore in this price range the demand curve is _____

    D. At a price of $4 total revenue is _____\
       At a price of $5 total revenue is _____\
       Therefore in this price range the demand curve is _____

    E. At a price of $5 total revenue is _____\
       At a price of $6 total revenue is _____\
       Therefore in this price range the demand curve is _____

    F. At a price of $6 total revenue is _____\
       At a price of $7 total revenue is _____\
       Therefore in this price range the demand curve is _____

    G. At a price of $7 total revenue is _____\
       At a price of $8 total revenue is _____\
       Therefore in this price range the demand curve is _____

    H. At a price of $8 total revenue is _____\
       At a price of $9 total revenue is _____\
       Therefore in this price range the demand curve is _____

    I. At a price of $9 total revenue is _____\
       At a price of $10 total revenue is _____\
       Therefore in this price range the demand curve is _____

2. List all price ranges in which demand is elastic.

3. List all price ranges in which demand is inelastic.

4. Are there any price ranges in which demand is neither elastic nor inelastic? If so, what label applies to the elasticity of demand in those price ranges?

5. What is true about marginal revenue when demand is elastic?

6. What is true about marginal revenue when demand is inelastic?

7. What is true about marginal revenue when demand is unit elastic?

Chapter 5
FACTOR MARKETS

....

Classroom Experiment 5.A

Deriving the Labor Supply Curve: Put Your Hands Up

Time Required: *10 - 15 minutes*	***Materials***: *none*	***Level of Difficulty:*** *low to moderate*
Purpose: *to derive a labor supply curve and provide insight into the market for labor.*	***Textbook Coverage of Underlying Topics***: *Explorations in Economics*: Chapter 11	

INTRODUCTION

The demand curve for labor is derived by simply multiplying the marginal product of labor (as you may have derived yourself in the Econville Links Experiment, activity 4.A) by the marginal revenue (which is equivalent to the price for competitive firms) earned from sales of the good being produced. In this experiment we will derive a labor supply curve in a straightforward manner. As potential or actual labor market participants ourselves, it is not difficult for us to think about the wage that would get us to work at all, or to work more than we do. Given the available wages and employment opportunities, we regularly face decisions about how much to work. This experiment will make use of what may be well-thought-out thresholds for your willingness to work.

SCENARIOS

In some employment settings, such as those involving migrant farm workers, foremen come before groups of potential workers and call out increasing wage offers until enough laborers step forward to meet the employer's needs. This experiment will be similar, except that the number of workers willing to provide a day's work will be recorded for each wage, with no goals in terms of the total number of workers willing to work. For the purposes of the experiment, imagine that you are considering employment at the local pizzeria.

Scenario 1. Suppose that besides the pizza shop, the other employment opportunities are no different than the opportunities you presently face in reality. Think for a moment or two, and then write down the lowest amount of money that the pizza shop could pay you to make pizzas for them this Saturday from 8 A.M. to 5 P.M. with a one-hour lunch. This is a daily wage, not an hourly wage. (Assume that this lowest amount will not affect the actual amount that you receive, so there is no benefit in overstating the minimum you would accept.)

Scenario 2. Now imagine that in addition to the other things you could be doing on Saturday, your favorite television program will air its season finale in mid-afternoon. What is the lowest amount they could pay you to work from 8 A.M.– 5 P.M. on Saturday?

Scenario 3. As a last scenario, suppose that your favorite TV program will NOT be on this Saturday but that you just wrecked your car, and within 30 days you must pay $1000 towards higher insurance rates, damage deductibles, and moving violation fines. What is the lowest payment that would motivate you to want to work this Saturday from 8 A.M. to 8 P.M.?

The numbers you have written down are called *reservation wages*, meaning that you would work for those amounts or anything more, but you would not work for anything less than those amounts. Now, as your instructor/foreman calls out various daily wages for working in the pizza shop, raise your hand (the one you don't write with) the first time the daily wage *equals or exceeds* your reservation wage. For example, if your reservation wage is $13, raise your hand when your foreman says $15. With your other hand, record the total number of people willing to work at each wage. This is the sum of those willing to work at the previous wage and the new workers added at the current wage.

WAGE	TOTAL WORKERS SCENARIO 1	TOTAL WORKERS SCENARIO 2	TOTAL WORKERS SCENARIO 3
0	_____	_____	_____
5	_____	_____	_____
10	_____	_____	_____
15	_____	_____	_____
20	_____	_____	_____
25	_____	_____	_____
30	_____	_____	_____
35	_____	_____	_____
40	_____	_____	_____
45	_____	_____	_____
50	_____	_____	_____
55	_____	_____	_____
60	_____	_____	_____
65	_____	_____	_____
70	_____	_____	_____
75	_____	_____	_____
80	_____	_____	_____
85	_____	_____	_____
90	_____	_____	_____
95	_____	_____	_____
100	_____	_____	_____

Favorite Ways to Explore Economics

REFLECTIONS
(Please answer these questions *after* completing the classroom experiment.)

1. On the diagram below, graph the labor market supply curves for each of the scenarios.

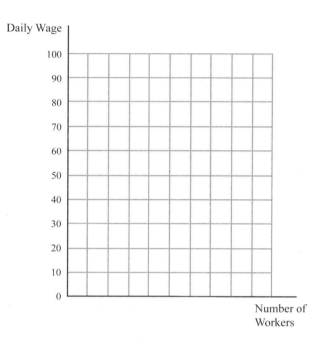

2. Why do you suppose some people had lower reservation wages than others?

3. Describe what happened to your reservation wage in Scenario 2 relative to Scenario 1 and why. Did your classmates behave similarly?

4. Describe what happened to your reservation wage in Scenario 3 relative to Scenario 1 and why. Did your classmates behave similarly?

5. Relative to Scenario 1, what happened to the number of workers supplied at most wage levels in Scenario 2? Can you think of another influence that might have a similar effect on the market labor supply curve?

6. Relative to Scenario 1, what happened to the number of workers supplied at most wage levels in Scenario 3? Can you think of another influence that might have a similar effect on the market labor supply curve?

AFTERTHOUGHTS

In the real labor market, the decision of whether or not to work on a given day is complicated by opportunities to work part-time, full-time, overtime, and sometimes (particularly for the self-employed) exactly how many hours to work. There may also be flexibility in the number of days worked. Nonetheless, the labor supply curve is constructed just as you have done so—the total amount of labor that workers are willing to supply is graphed at each possible wage. Equilibrium in the labor market is achieved at the intersection of this curve and the labor market demand curve.

For a more in-depth labor market experiment, see Michael J. Haupert's "Labor Market Experiment," *Journal of Economic Education*, Fall 1990, p. 300.

Classroom Experiment 5.B

Learning from Teaching: The Anti-REM Game

Time Required: *30 minutes*   **Materials**: *none*   **Level of Difficulty:** *moderate*

Purpose: *to reinforce difficult concepts by*   **Textbook Coverage of Underlying Topics**:
having students teach them to each other.   *Explorations in Economics:* Chapter 11

INTRODUCTION

This game grew out of the authors' belief that just as there is REM (rapid eye movement) sleep, there is REM (really elsewhere mode) class participation. The authors of this book have spent many thousands of hours in class. Believe us, we can daydream with the best of them. When you're concentrating more on an upcoming vacation, meal, or social interaction than on an important lecture, the Anti-REM game is the antidote.

SCENARIO

You will be randomly paired with a classmate for this exercise. One member of each pair will go outside the classroom and think deep thoughts or quietly discuss how to save (conquer?) the world for five minutes or so while the other member of each pair learns a new and exciting economics topic. When the ousted half of each pair is invited back into the classroom, it is the task of the learned half to teach their ousted partners the concept they just learned. After five minutes or so of intensive teaching and learning, the ousted crew that was taught by the learned few will be asked to respond to a few questions on the material.

REFLECTIONS
(Please answer these questions *after* completing the classroom experiment.)

1. What is the concept you learned and why is it important?

2. Do incentives matter? In other words, how did your obligation to teach or be tested on the material affect your attention to the material being presented?

3. Assuming that those who became student-teachers learned the economic content of the exercise better than the average student trying to learn from passive reading and lectures, how could you alter your typical study routine to reap the same benefits?

AFTERTHOUGHTS

With luck you have learned two valuable lessons from this exercise. First, you have obtained a solid understanding of an important economic concept. And second, you have picked up a new tool for your bag of learning tricks. Instructors know well that teaching a concept is a great way to force yourself to learn it. When you know you have to explain something to others, you don't let yourself get away with skimming and partial comprehension. Sometimes even explaining something to yourself, as you can when you take notes in your own words on concepts explained in your textbook, will solidify ideas and allow difficult ideas to fit together in a way that just can't happen while you're daydreaming about fudge brownies.

Favorite Ways to Explore Economics

Problem Set 5.1

Total Product and Marginal Product

The following table lists the quantity of output produced by the Julienne Factory.

QUANTITY OF LABOR	TOTAL OUTPUT	MARGINAL PRODUCT OF LABOR
0	0	
1	100	_____
2	350	_____
3	550	_____
4	650	_____
5	700	_____
6	700	_____
7	650	_____
8	550	_____

1. Fill in the blanks in the table.

2. Plot the total product of labor curve on the graph below.

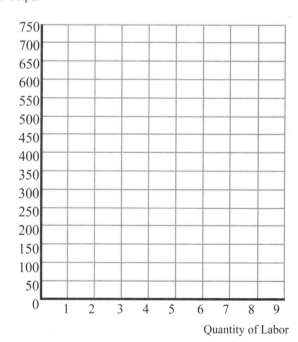

Quantity of Output

Quantity of Labor

3. Plot the marginal product of labor curve on the graph below.

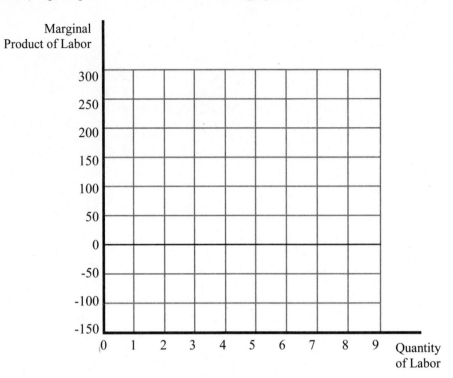

4. At what point do diminishing marginal returns set in?

5. How were you able to determine where diminishing marginal returns set in?

Problem Set 5.2

More on Marginal Product

The following table is for a perfectly competitive firm.

QUANTITY OF LABOR	TOTAL OUTPUT	MARGINAL PRODUCT OF LABOR
0	0	
1	5	
2	15	
3	30	
4	40	
5	45	
6	45	
7	40	

1. Calculate the additional output (marginal product) attributable to each worker and fill in the blanks in the table with these numbers.

2. At what point (if any) do diminishing returns set in? How were you able to determine that?

3. If this product sells for $5.00 each, calculate the value of the marginal product of labor in the table below.

QUANTITY OF LABOR	VALUE OF THE MARGINAL PRODUCT
0	
1	_____
2	_____
3	_____
4	_____
5	_____
6	_____
7	_____

4. If each worker receives a wage of $40.00, how many workers will a profit maximizing firm hire? Why?

5. If the product price were to increase to $10.00 each how would that affect the answer to question 4?

Problem Set 5.3

Derived Demand

Complete the following table for a perfectly competitive firm.

QUANTITY OF LABOR	TOTAL OUTPUT	MARGINAL PRODUCT	PRODUCT PRICE	VALUE OF MARGINAL PRODUCT
0	0		$5.00	
1	5	_____	_____	_____
2	15	_____	_____	_____
3	30	_____	_____	_____
4	40	_____	_____	_____
5	45	_____	_____	_____
6	45	_____	_____	_____

1. Fill in the blanks in the table.

2. The value of the marginal product of labor is the demand for labor. The value of the margina product of labor is the marginal product of labor times the product price. Plot the demand for labor on the graph to the right.

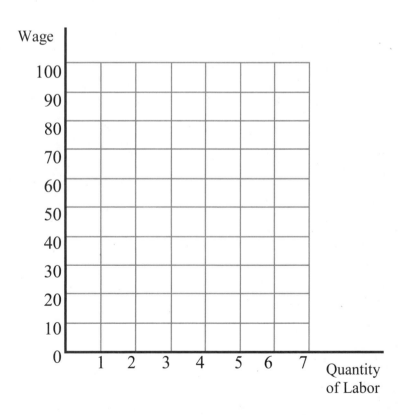

3. Indicate what (if anything) would happen to the demand for labor after each of the following:

A. An increase in worker productivity

B. An increase in the popularity of the product

C. A decrease in worker motivation and interest in the job

D. The introduction of new technology that makes workers able to produce more in a given amount of time

E. A decrease in the price of the product

Problem Set 5.4

Changing Marginal Product and Product Price

1. Use economic terminology to explain how a worker training program that increased the productivity of labor would affect the demand for labor.

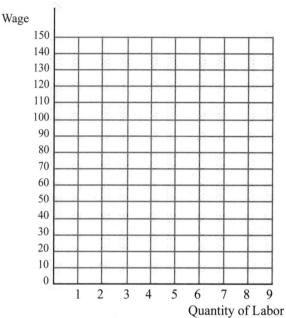

2. Suppose that starting with the data from Problem Set 5.3, workers become twice as productive after completing a training program. Calculate the new value of their marginal product. Complete the table below and re-graph the old demand for labor along with the new demand for labor that would result from the change in productivity.

QUANTITY OF LABOR	TOTAL OUTPUT		MARGINAL PRODUCT		PRODUCT PRICE	VALUE OF MARGINAL PRODUCT	
	(OLD)	(NEW)	(OLD)	(NEW)		(OLD)	(NEW)
0	0						
1	5		5		5		
2	15		10		5		
3	30		15		5		
4	40		10		5		
5	45		5		5		
6	45		0		5		
7	40		-5		5		

3. How would an increase in the price of the product being sold affect the demand for labor?

4. Starting with the original marginal product numbers from Problem Set 5.3, calculate the effect of an increase in the product price from $5.00 to $7.50. Complete the table below and re-graph the old demand for labor along with the new demand for labor that would result from the price change.

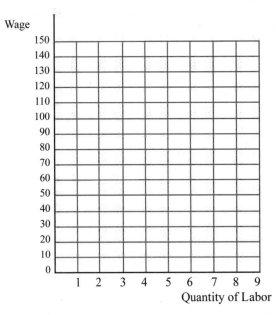

QUANTITY OF LABOR	MARGINAL PRODUCT	PRODUCT PRICE		VALUE OF MARGINAL PRODUCT	
		(OLD)	(NEW)	(OLD)	(NEW)
0		5			
1	5	5			
2	10	5			
3	15	5			
4	10	5			
5	5	5			
6	0	5			
7	-5	5			

Problem Set 5.5

The Unemployment Rate and the Minimum Wage

Use the information in the graph below to answer the following questions. Please refer to the letters provided along the horizontal axis when discussing quantities of labor.

1. What is the quantity of labor employed at the equilibrium wage?

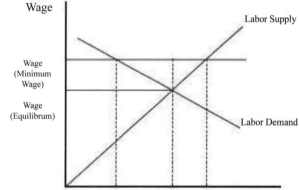

2. If a minimum wage is set at Wage (minimum wage), what would be the quantity of labor demanded?

3. If a minimum wage is set at Wage (minimum wage), what would be the quantity of labor supplied?

4. How many people would become unemployed as a result of the minimum wage?

5. Of those who became unemployed, how many had a job and then lost that job as a result of the minimum wage?

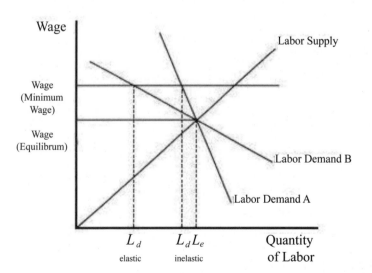

6. Referring to the graph to the right, if a minimum wage is imposed as shown, how will its effect be different if the demand for labor is represented by Labor Demand A versus Labor Demand B?

7. Opponents of a minimum wage law would argue that the demand for labor more closely resembles which labor demand curve?

8. Proponents of a minimum wage law would argue that the demand for labor more closely resembles which labor demand curve?

Chapter 6
THE PUBLIC SECTOR AND MARKET FAILURE
••

Classroom Experiment 6.A

Free Rider Experiment: Show Me the Money

Time Required: 10 minutes	***Materials***: recording sheets (scrap paper)	***Level of Difficulty:*** low
Purpose: to demonstrate the temptation to free ride and the trouble it creates.	***Textbook Coverage of Underlying Topics***: *Explorations in Economics:* Chapter 9	

INTRODUCTION

This experiment speaks to the appropriate treatment of public goods. Public goods are those which no one can be excluded from using, and whose values to any particular user are not diminished by the goods' use by other users. National defense and lighthouses are classic examples. Once a lighthouse is erected, no ship can be prevented from benefiting from its guidance, and use of the lighthouse by one ship does not detract from its use by other ships. Most goods, like chocolate bars, are not public goods—you can exclude others from eating your chocolate, and if you eat your chocolate bar, its value to others is certainly diminished. However, many important goods, like TV and radio signals, police and fire protection, parks, roads, and street lights, fall into the realm of public goods. They may not all be perfect examples, as roads can be blocked to prevent entry and parks can fill up, but they share the non-rival and nonexcludable characteristics at least up to a point.

SCENARIO

Your instructor has credited your fictional bank account with $10 worth of funny money. This will buy you nothing, but it gives you pleasure just knowing that you have it (especially if you have more than your neighbor). Being a kind and generous person, your instructor has agreed to double any amount of money that is invested in his or her "doubling pool," and divide this doubled amount among everyone in the class. All students receive an equal share of the doubled pool regardless of their investment or lack thereof. You can invest any amount from 0 to $10 (no change please) to be doubled. Record the amount you want to invest on the small investment recording slip (A.K.A. scrap paper) provided by your instructor and hand it in at the designated time. Your instructor will add up all of the investments, double them, and divide that amount by the number of students in the class. If a total of $150 is invested and there are 20 students in the class, the $150 becomes $300 when doubled and this is divided among 20 students to obtain the $15 share for each student. Those who invested $10 will end up with a total of $15.

Those who invested nothing will get $15 to add to the $10 they kept for a total of $25. If everyone invested $10, everyone would end up with $20. You may discuss contributions with your classmates prior to making your investment decisions, but the actual investment amounts will be collected anonymously so that no one knows the strategy of any other particular person.

REFLECTIONS
(Please answer these questions *after* completing the classroom experiment.)

1. What strategy for the class would maximize the total amount of money received by each student?

2. Did you follow that strategy? If not, why not?

3. Did your class experience a free-rider problem, meaning that students attempted to benefit from the investments of others without contributing their fair share?

4. Other than the goods mentioned in the description of this experiment, list at least two other goods that might face similar free-rider problems when people try to collect money to fund them in real life.

5. What role could government play in providing the socially optimal quantity of public goods while avoiding the free-rider problem?

6. Some people do make voluntary donations to help fund public or nearly public goods like National Public Radio, the Public Broadcasting System, churches, and community centers. What could explain this behavior?

AFTERTHOUGHTS

Those trying to collect contributions to pay for public goods, like neighborhood groups collecting for a central flower display, often experience free rider problems because citizens can benefit from the public good whether or not they contribute. Similarly, investment in this experiment's doubling pool invited free riding. By not investing, students obtained the benefits from others' investments while holding on to their own money. In both cases, even though the benefits to society exceed the cost of investment, each person's selfish incentive is to contribute nothing. The outcome is a form of market failure that results in less than the socially optimal quantity of these goods being produced and consumed. Note that unlike other types of goods, since many people can benefit from the *same* unit of a public good, the additional or "marginal" benefit from one more unit of a public good is determined by adding up the marginal benefit to each member of society who would benefit from that unit.

Classroom Experiment 6.B

Tragedy of the Commons Game: Where the Moose Roam

Time Required: 20 minutes	*Materials*: 1 herd of moose (supplied by your instructor, for those not in the North)	*Level of Difficulty:* low to moderate. Players make decisions under uncertainty.
Purpose: to place students into the context of an open-access resource and allow them to experience the incentives provided by differing solutions.	*Textbook Coverage of Underlying Topics*: *Explorations in Economics:* Chapter 9	

INTRODUCTION

As your economics course continues, you will learn not only the workings of markets, but the critical importance of various components of our economic system. This activity will shed light on the roles of government and property rights in reconciling the supply and demand of exploitable resources.

SCENARIO

You are a meat and fur trader in the rugged North. As you hunt moose, you are aware of the following facts:

- Each hunting season lasts 30 seconds.
- If there are fewer than eight moose, reproduction will not occur (for lack of genetic and gender diversity).
- If there are more than eight moose, the number of moose will double after each hunting season. That is, if 10 moose remain after a hunting season, there will be 20 moose the next hunting season.
- When hunting, you care only about the number of moose, and not about age or location.
- Despite the fact that moose appear cuddly and cute, so are your spouse and child, and this is the only means by which to feed and clothe them. Thus, you want to maximize your "harvest."
- Finally, you plan to be around for many more periods, and you do not know how many more hunting seasons remain.

Other aspects of the scenario will change over the periods, as indicated by your instructor. In each of the periods, examine your interests and incentives and then make the "best" choice in regard to your moose harvest.

REFLECTIONS
(Please answer these questions *after* completing the classroom experiment.)

1. What is the role of property rights in the allocation of moose?

2. Great philosophers like John Locke have argued that government is necessary to provide for property ownership. Give specific examples of the roles government plays in assigning and enforcing property rights.

3. Are there places on your school's campus that suffer from the tragedy of the commons—in other words, the lack of well defined property rights?

4. Are there existing problems in society that could be solved if only we could better assign property rights? If so, provide some examples.

AFTERTHOUGHTS

Moose hunting aside, the lesson you just learned applies to everything from radio waves to the open sea. Ownership of the former has been assigned, much like property rights, to prevent broadcasters from trampling upon each other's frequencies. The oceans are harder to monitor, not to mention the difficulty of finding agreement over property rights among the many nations bordering the sea. As our experiment would predict, private land, livestock, and radio wave frequencies are well cared for, while problems with excess pollution and over-hunting in open-access areas persist.

Problem Set 6.1

Tax Incidence

Local authorities view the production of "Famous Economist Trading Cards" as a threat to the welfare of Econville's citizenry. To limit risk exposure, they levy a tax on the manufacture of these cards in hopes that it will discourage consumption. The following graph demonstrates the supply and demand for "Famous Economist Trading Cards," taking into account the private cost and benefit of their production

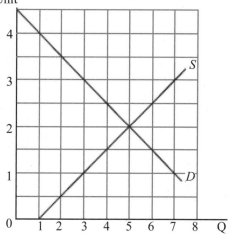

1. Identify the equilibrium price and quantity of "Famous Economist Trading Cards."

2. On the graph demonstrate the effect of imposing a $1.00 per card tax on the production of the cards.

3. Identify the new price that consumers pay and the price producers receive after paying the tax.

4. Compare your answers to 1 and 3 above and comment on who bears the burden (or incidence) of this tax.

5. Repeat questions 1-4 for the following graphs.

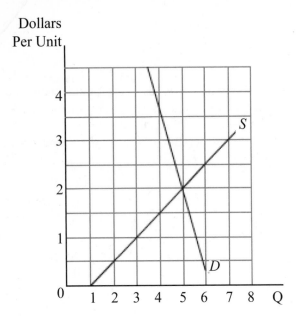

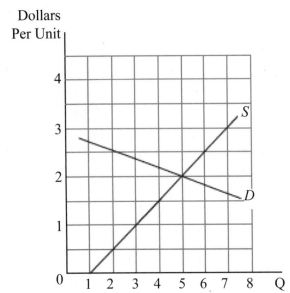

6. What can you conclude about the relationship between tax incidence and the demand for the good being taxed?

Problem Set 6.2

Progressivity

In the country of Econville there are four states, Microland, Macroland, Tradeland, and Consumerland. Each of these states has its own state tax system. In the table below are the taxes for each of the states.

INCOME	MICROLAND TAX	MACROLAND TAX	TRADELAND TAX	CONSUMERLAND TAX
$10,000	$1,000	$1,000	$1,000	$1,000
$20,000	$1,000	$2,000	$1,250	$2,500
$30,000	$1,000	$3,000	$1,500	$4,250
$40,000	$1,000	$4,000	$1,750	$6,500
$50,000	$1,000	$5,000	$2,000	$9,500

1. Classify the tax structures of each of the states as being either progressive, proportional, or regressive.

2. Explain in each case how you were able to classify the tax system of each state.

Problem Set 6.3

Positive Externalities

 Phillipo Epstein loved fireworks and wanted to organize numerous fireworks shows for the benefit of his community each year. He asked all the residents of his community to anonymously indicate the value they would place on each of 20 fireworks shows he could put on in a year. He used that information to graph the community demand curve provided below. As indicated by the marginal cost curve, each show would cost the community $10,000. That worked out to $10 for each of the 1,000 residents. After analyzing the graph, Phillipo concluded that he should put on 12 shows. However, when Phillipo asked each resident to pay his or her $120 share of the cost of 12 shows, Phillipo was shocked and horrified to find that none of the residents wanted to contribute. The most honest residents admitted that they hoped to watch shows paid for by other people, but would avoid paying for the shows themselves if possible.

1. Was Phillipo correct in identifying the optimal quantity of fireworks shows as 12? Explain your answer.

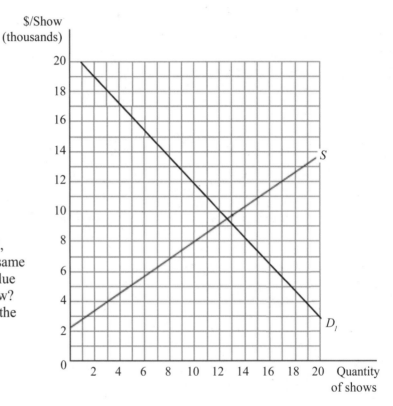

2. Suppose the residents were identical, meaning that each resident placed the same value on any particular show. What value did each resident place on the first show? What value did each resident place on the 12th show? Explain your answer.

3. If each resident hoped to free ride on the fireworks shows purchased by others, and each refused to pay anything for a fireworks show, what would each resident's demand curve look like?

4. What characteristics make a good or service such as fireworks shows a public good?

5. What can you conclude about the likelihood of private markets providing the optimal quantity of events such as fireworks shows?

6. Explain one solution that would lead to the optimal provision of goods and services such as fireworks displays.

7. What are some other examples of goods and services that involve a free-rider problem?

Problem Set 6.4

Negative Externalities

A company has decided to locate its new textbook manufacturing plant on the local river. Effluent from the production process is released into the river. When questioned about this practice, the company responded that it is cheaper to release waste into the river than to have it hauled away. In the weeks that followed, much discussion took place and eventually the local authorities decided to impose a $25 per unit tax on this company.

The following graph shows the supply and demand curves for the plant.

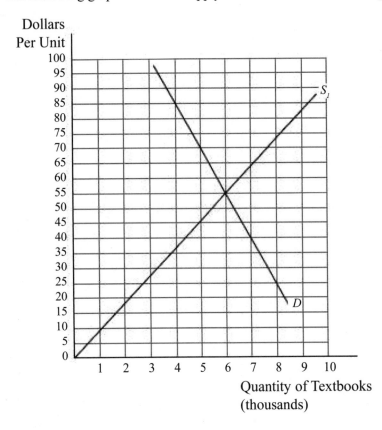

1. Identify the equilibrium price and quantity for textbooks from the plant.

2. Calculate the new supply (with the imposition of the tax) and plot it on the above graph.

3. Identify the new quantity demanded.

4. If it is true that the original supply curve depicts the private cost of producing textbooks given the ability to release effluent into the river, and that the new supply curve (including the tax) depicts the social cost of producing textbooks, what cost do people not associated with the production or consumption of textbooks pay per textbook produced?

5. What is the resource allocation problem associated with the presence of significant negative externalities?

6. Explain one market-based solution that would correct for this misallocation of resources.

7. What are some other examples of activities that create negative externalities? How would you suggest that we correct for the resulting market failure?

Problem Set 6.5

Congested Parks – A Pricing Dilemma[1]

This reading provides a worthwhile overview of supply, demand, and efficiency issues in the context of environmental affairs, and serves as the basis for the problems that follow. Some sections involve economic concepts that you have not yet covered, and serve to foreshadow and motivate upcoming material.

Our national parks, along with many state and local recreation areas, strain to accommodate ever-increasing numbers of visitors. It is easy to conclude that these congestion difficulties justify the creation of new public parks, and expanded outdoor recreation facilities in existing ones. Additions to supply would seem appropriate, considering the rising demand. Yet, the apparently inadequate capacities of various public parks may reflect something other than a lag in the adjustment of supply to growing demand. Governments may be distorting the recreation market by charging too little for the recreational use of public parks. Such an improper pricing practice could lead to the misallocation of resources. Some groups would benefit—perhaps those that are not intended to—at the expense of others. Economic analysis helps to show the nature and probable consequences of the park crowding problem.

When Demand Crowds Supply

Overflowing visitation at a public park provides a textbook display of a shortage. Park crowding means insufficient park space—or types of park space, such as camping space, driving space, fishing space, etc.—to satisfy outdoor recreationists. They want more. Their wants, however, depend directly on what they must pay. The existence of a shortage says only that the quantity demanded exceeds the quantity supplied at the going price. Excessive park crowding, therefore, reflects a park entry or a park privilege fee that is below the one that equates the amount of park space consumers want to the amount available.

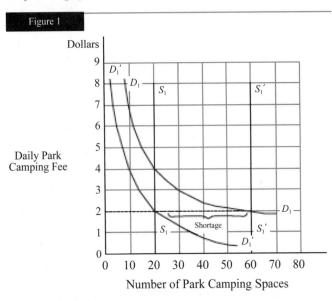

Figure 1

Figure 1 shows a set of demand and supply relationships for camping spaces in a hypothetical public park. Demand curve D_1D_1 shows that the lower the price, the larger the number of identical park camping spaces desired on an average summer day. Vertical line S_1S_1 indicates the number of camping spaces in the park, assumed to be an invariable quantity in the short run. Suppose park officials set the camping fee at $2. Quantity demanded (60 spaces) exceeds quantity supplied (20 spaces), so a shortage of 40 spaces prevails at that price.

What happens to the 40 camping families whom the park cannot accommodate? Those who can return home may disappointedly do so. Others may not show up, having heard about or previously experienced the shortage. Still others may try to squeeze and shoehorn into the camping area, or pitch their tents in unauthorized areas of the park. Some may find other public or private places to camp nearby. The remainder may stay in motels, sleep along the road, or drive all night.

---

[1] Adapted from: Monthly Review, St. Louis Federal Reserve, Dan M. Bechter.

As can be seen, selling a good or service below the market-clearing price—where demand equals supply, or $4, in the example—simply requires other forms of rationing or adjustment, such as first come, first served, which places a premium on arrival time. Some of these adaptations, in effect, increase the cost of the outdoor recreation experience. They make the consumer spend extra time and money for participation in the leisure activity. Other adjustments, such as crowding into available space, make outdoor recreation less fun.

The shortage shown in Figure 1—or any market shortage for that matter—can be reduced by (a) increasing price; (b) increasing supply; (c) decreasing demand; or (d) a combination of the preceding. Before considering these solutions, consider a part of what is going on outside the park.

Figure 2 shows another set of supply and demand curves—those for camping spaces on private land near the hypothetical public park. Currently, entrepreneurs are making 18 such spaces available and charging the market price of $2.50. Note that quantity demanded equals quantity supplied at this price; there is no shortage here. On a day of normal demand, everyone who wants to camp in a private area can do so. Some of the demand for private camping space depends, of course, on overflow from the public park.

Assuming that campers prefer locations within the park to those outside, it might seem strange that some are willing to pay the extra half dollar charged by private campgrounds. It must be remembered, however, that the park cannot satisfy demand at $2. Also, note that a sizable portion of the left tail of demand curve D_1D_1 in Figure 1 lies above the $4 price line, indicating that several campers are willing to pay more than this amount for places inside the park. Some of these people certainly would be willing to locate outside for less when the park is full.

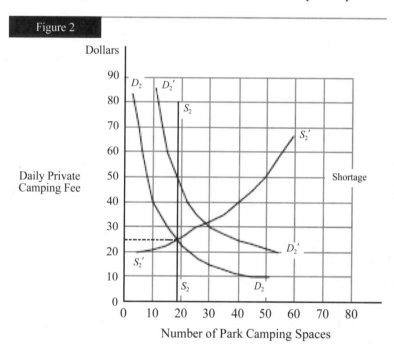

Figure 2

Now, consider each of the solutions to the shortage of public park camping spaces. Suppose first that the park authorities raise their camping fee to $4. We see in Figure 1 that the shortage immediately disappears. Everyone wanting a space within the park at this price finds one, because quantity demanded declines from 60 to 20 spaces. In addition, because of the increase in the park's camping fee, more people will decide in favor of the less expensive private facilities. Demand curve D_2D_2 for private camping spaces (Figure 2) will shift over to $D_2'D_2'$. For a while, there will be a shortage of private camping spaces, and campground owners may raise their prices. Eventually they will expand, or new private campgrounds will open. This is what curve $S_2'S_2'$ shows—the number of camping spaces private landowners will supply, given the opportunity to adjust to various prices. As we see, the market price settles at just over $30 a space, where quantity demanded equals quantity supplied at 29 spaces. ($S_2'S_2'$ slopes upward to the right, showing that costs per space increase as space is increased.) Furthermore, the market for motel rooms, among other related markets, will be affected.

Suppose that instead of increasing price, the park officials increase the number of camping spaces from 20 to 60, shifting supply out to $S_1'S_1'$ in Figure 1. Again, the shortage disappears. As a result, however, the private campgrounds receive less business. (In Figure 2, D_2D_2 shifts left—not shown.) The markets for hotels among other substitutes and complements are affected, too.

Instead of increasing the number or price of camping spaces in the existing park, authorities could alleviate the crowding problem by reducing the demand for these spaces. (D_1D_1 would shift left to $D_1'D_1'$ in Figure 1.) They could achieve this by allowing the quality of the park facilities to decrease, opening additional parks, or subsidizing private campgrounds to lower their costs and encourage their expansion and improvement.

Each of these alternatives affects the outdoor recreation market differently. If camping conditions in the public park are allowed to deteriorate, for example, the demand for private campground space in the vicinity might rise as the desirability of these private areas increases relative to those in the park. On the other hand, the region may become less attractive as an outdoor recreation area, especially if the whole park deteriorates, and private enterprise also may suffer declines in demand. Creating more public parks or subsidizing private outdoor recreation areas in the region should decrease demand for space in individual parks, at least in the short run. It could also make the whole area more attractive as a recreation destination and thereby increase demand for all of the parks in the long run.

How Many People? How Much per Person?

Since undue crowding caused by an economic shortage can be eliminated by increasing the price, one wonders why this quick and obvious solution is not chosen. Alternatively, when "idle" space seems plentiful in the park, why not develop it for the more intensive recreational purposes that consumers want? Clearly, certain obstacles must he barring the wholesale use of these prescriptions. Indeed, several less apparent economic considerations make it difficult to determine the desirable amount of park use. Still other socioeconomic factors affect decisions of how to best allocate this use among outdoor recreationists.

Principles of Private Pricing

As a starting point, it proves helpful to think of how a public park would be managed if it were a privately owned enterprise. Microeconomic analysis proceeds from the axiom that an individual economic unit behaves in ways that it believes to be in its own self-interest. The theory of the firm treats profits as a measure of self-interest, and economists have found that the simple assumption that business enterprises act to maximize profits explains much of firm behavior. Assume that this objective—profit maximization—guides the park managers. Under such an assumption, what can one expect?

The owners may conclude that their land and water holdings would yield higher profits if used for purposes other than, or in addition to, outdoor recreation. With profit maximization as their goal, they may choose to turn the park into a farm, a strip mine, an oil field, or a residential area. Is this bad? Maybe, but the free country, free market philosophy argues that consumers, with their dollar votes, should direct the use of resources. In an idealized economic system, higher profit levels serve to stimulate production of those goods and services that society wants most. However, market imperfections such as its inability to incorporate external pollution costs, and an excessive discounting of the value of resources to future generations, leave our economy well shy of this idealized state. Consequently, profit signals cannot always be relied on to allocate resources in society's best interest, not to mention the best interest of other living things.

In the absence of such shortcomings, the most profitable use of resources would presumably be the most economically desirable. Thus, if private interests would operate resources differently from the government, the public use may have a questionable economic basis. The government should be able to defend its choice of uses by establishing the presence of considerations not fully reflected in profits and by showing that including these considerations favors using the resources in a less profitable manner.

Otherwise—putting this back into context—if the government cannot show that the net economic benefits of a public park at least equal those society receives by allowing the same area of land and water to be operated for the top competing purpose, the park cannot be justified.

Note that in choosing from alternative uses of resources, it is wrong to say that "other factors besides economics must be considered." Economics is the study of choices among competing alternatives. When making such choices, it is appropriate *within* economic analysis to consider all of the relevant factors, whether or not they involve money. The trick is to identify and include all of the relevant economic considerations, both current and future, when calculating benefits and costs. Confusion arises because many people commonly but incorrectly use the word "economics" as if it were synonymous with "profits," or "private enterprise." For example, a television special about a national park reported that the reconsideration of plans for a new airport represented a victory for conservation over economics. That was not the case. It represented a reassessment of the net benefits from building the airport. Society decided that it would be worse off—all things considered—with the airport, and so the decision not to build it was a wise choice in terms of both economics and conservation.

Returning to the question of pricing, suppose that businessmen do operate the parkland as an outdoor recreation area. To keep things simple, let the rental of camping spaces be the park's sole market activity. The profit maximizing owners will need to know (a) the demand for their camping spaces, and (b) the amount it costs them to supply varying numbers of camping spaces.

Complexities appear quickly. The relationship between price and quantity demanded is complicated by the fact that the quality of the product depends on the number of people buying it. Up to a point, the representative camper may enjoy the camping experience more as the number of other campers in the park increases. He likes their company. Eventually, however, increases in the number of campers reduce the camper's total satisfaction. He dislikes crowding. Assuming the quality of camping first rises and then falls with the number of campers, so does the amount the camper is willing to pay (Figure 3).

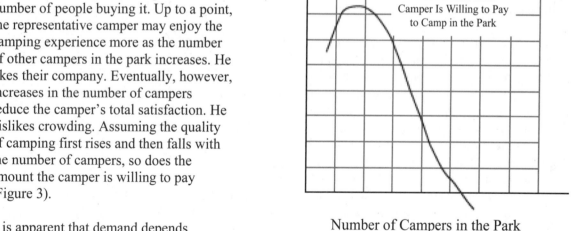

Figure 3

It is apparent that demand depends implicitly on supply. In the short run, a fixed amount of parkland cannot supply various quantities of constant-quality camping spaces. Campers want more than just a place to sleep. They also want open, natural spaces around them. When more camping spaces are supplied, less open space remains. Because of the crowding phenomenon, quantity demanded may become unresponsive to reductions in price once certain degrees of congestion are reached. Rational profit-maximizing park owners would never reduce price under such circumstances.

In their cost calculation, the park owners will allow for upkeep. As more camping spaces are rented, the cost of maintaining each additional space may decline as certain economies are realized. On the other hand, the least expensive ways of supplying camping spaces may be exhausted early. Also, as the number of camping spaces grows, the cost of maintaining the quality (of the decreased quantity) of open space might increase, perhaps dramatically, as certain critical levels of camping pressure are reached. For example, the park's wildlife—a prime attraction to campers—may cease to reproduce without sufficient space and seclusion.

Taking all internal cost and demand considerations into account, owners maximize profits by choosing price and quantity such that further reductions in price would increase revenues from camping space rentals by less than the cost of supplying these additional spaces.

Principles of Public Pricing

Parks often possess unique features and are located unequal distances from the homes of their visitors. This product differentiation implies that each park faces a downward-sloping demand curve. Under such monopolistically competitive conditions, owners must reduce prices on all spaces in order to rent more spaces, and thus the additional or marginal revenue from renting one more camping space is less than the price at which it is rented. Profits decline with increased "sales" once marginal cost exceeds marginal revenue, and therefore profits are below their maximum at the higher quantity where price equals marginal cost. For the economy as a whole, economic efficiency requires that resources be used until the marginal social benefit of each resulting good or service equals its marginal social cost. If all of society's costs of park use are borne by the park owners, and if all of society's benefits of park use are received by the park visitors, it follows that the profit-maximizing price will limit park use more than is desirable. Private owners will stop short of the point where the resource cost of supplying that last camping space exactly equals what society is willing to pay for it.

This leads directly to the obvious but important corollary: *Under conditions of monopolistic competition where all costs and benefits of park use are internal (that is, felt by those who create the costs and benefits), the socially optimal amount of park congestion exceeds that which would be permitted by unregulated private enterprise.* People may complain of crowded conditions in a public park, but that *in itself* does not justify limits on visitation. So long as the discomforts of crowding are internalized—that is, so long as visitors would accept them in exchange for the correspondingly low prices—the park visitor (assuming she or he fully anticipates the situation) has no economic grounds for complaint.

People who do not visit a park may benefit from those who do. Juvenile delinquency, for example, may be reduced by providing city park and recreation areas. These external benefits might justify a subsidy—a payment to those who use the park. It sounds strange, but why not? If, for example, it is found that children who participate in little league baseball are less likely to get sick, less likely to turn to crime, and less likely to go on welfare, might it not make sense to expand such programs even if it requires giving the participants some monetary inducement? Nonvisitors also may benefit from a park's provision of natural habitat for wildlife, its protection of rare plants and animals, and its preservation of unique natural and historical areas. Birds that nest in a park, for example, fly, feed, and sing far outside its boundaries. Benefits are sometimes less obvious. Relatively few people have ever seen a whooping crane, but millions derive pleasure from reading and hearing about its fight for survival. Conceivably, therefore, society's interest could be served by subsidizing park crowds, if not more parks.

On the other hand, the benefits that nonvisitors receive may be *inversely* related to the number of park visitors. The more people who drive to the park, for example, the more highway congestion and air pollution for everyone. Park wildlife can damage crops and otherwise increase the cost of farming and ranching. As already noted, greater visitor pressure can reduce park quality. To the extent that added visitation decreases the benefits that nonvisitors get from the park, park visits impose a cost on society. In the camping space example, external benefits of nonuse increase the economically appropriate price and decrease the desirable level of camping. If government officials ignore these external costs and benefits in their pricing of park services, society will not be best served.

A Pricing Dilemma

The theory of optimal pricing is, of course, far easier than its practice. It is one thing to say that all costs and benefits should be identified and measured, another to figure out how. These difficulties are important, but not the topic of concern here. Rather, this section focuses on an obstacle that keeps park officials from charging the economically appropriate price for park use even when that price is known— public opinion.

The conditions reported at some popular public parks do not suggest an equilibrium in quantity demanded and quantity supplied. True, as shown earlier in this article, congestion is sometimes economically desirable and can be expected to cause complaints of crowding. But when people are turned away and when overuse threatens the park's survival, something must be out of kilter. Park authorities seem to be both encouraging visitation with low fees, and discouraging visitation by not adequately expanding recreation facilities and by otherwise limiting—in nonprice fashions—the activities of the visitors.

Public opinion forces this strange behavior. In theory, at least, economists can usually fit public opinion into the pricing system by translating it into the dollar values that society places on the activities in question, like saving the bald eagle or cleaning up a polluted river. In this case, however, public opinion is against the pricing system. People strongly resist public park fees and the use of these fees to allocate park use. Americans apparently feel that public parks are theirs to use free of charge (or at nominal cost) as a right of part ownership. Strangely, they do not seem to feel this way about the Nation's highways (we have gasoline taxes as well as turnpike tolls). On highways too, however, improper pricing results in crowded conditions.

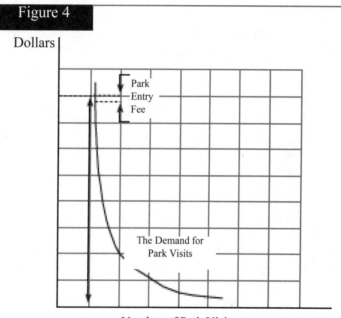

Figure 4

Related to the ownership argument is the redistributive argument that entry fees would have to be raised substantially to adequately limit visitation, and that this would discriminate against the poor. It might seem unlikely that the demand for a one-day park visit would be inelastic (meaning that price would have to go up by a lot to cause visitation to go down even by a little), but this may well be the case for parks like Yellowstone, because such large increases in entry fees may amount to relatively small percentage increases in the total cost of the park visit (Figure 4).

Until attitudes change, government officials face great resistance to increases in public park entry and use fees. Perhaps much of this resistance would decrease if proper pricing methods were used. Accelerating park deterioration and other costs of excessive crowding certainly call for changes in the pricing of park recreation. Paradoxically, governments appear to be working in the wrong direction. New highways to parks, for example, lower the time and money cost of a visit. The Annual Pass—an $80 annual permit that admits the purchaser and accompanying passengers to all national parks and Federal recreation sites— encourages more visitation.

Some groups, besides visitors, obviously benefit from park subsidies. Vested interests point to the regional activity generated by park use. Owners and employees of lodging places, restaurants, bait and tackle stores, and many other kinds of businesses and concessions do not want to give up what is actually a subsidy to them. They reason that, if parks increase fees, the demand for the complementary goods and services they sell will decline. Manufacturers of boats, automobiles, and other outdoor recreation equipment also benefit from the subsidization of park use.

Other groups suffer. It can be argued that the subsidization of park recreation reduces the demand for movies, bowling, and other activities that consumers consider substitutes. Ronald F. Lee writes "...for most people, there is no substitute for a visit to a national park."[2] A visit to a national park may be a unique experience, but that does not mean it has no substitutes. Most Americans already substitute other things—staying home, for example—for national park visits. And if the price of visiting national parks is increased, even more people will substitute other leisure activities.

Further Complexities and Ideas

Most public parks of any size supply several different types of outdoor recreation. Many of these compete with one another for available park space. One example of this has already been given: open space competes with park use. But water skiing competes with fishing, picnicking with camping, and so on. A park contains, therefore, several submarkets, and as such it can supply any one of many, many, different types of park use mixes. Some activities use more resources than others, and these should be priced higher. In practice, it may be extremely difficult and expensive to collect for each activity engaged in by a park visitor, but it might be possible to approximate his cost by charging him on the basis of the time he spends in the park and the equipment he takes in. Perhaps simply multiplying time by total vehicle weight by a price for a standard "user unit" would do the job. This would (1) discourage long stays, (2) discourage autos, campers, boats, and other heavy equipment, and (3) permit a relatively low entry price for visitors willing to travel light within the park and willing to stay only a short period. Some parks currently do not permit visitors to stay an indefinite periods of time. This is consistent with the philosophy that it is better for society if five people spend one day in the park than if one person spends five days. If this point of view is accepted, a fee rising *progressively* with length of stay is called for.

Seasonal park congestion could also be relieved by varying visitation fees by time of year. Although used to some extent, this method of pricing is largely untapped. The advance reservation idea probably favors certain groups over others, although it does have the advantage of guaranteeing space. Unfortunately, one likely outcome of a reservation system in situations where demand exceeds supply is a black market or scalper market in tickets. Why not use the pricing system directly instead of driving it underground?

The cost of park-type outdoor recreation must be borne by someone. This includes not only the direct operating costs, but also the opportunity costs of the resources and the external costs net of external benefits. If the public wants this kind of activity enough to pay for it, private enterprises will have every incentive to provide such parks. And, of course, there are many private enterprises of this nature now in existence.

The question is whether we should trust private enterprise to correct for market failure better than public institutions, and to preserve the natural beauty of the parks. Many park resources development decisions are irreversible, and the long-run consequences of a misguided short-run profit motive could be severe. On the other hand, public ownership does not guarantee development of resources in the long-run best interest of society either.

---

[2] *Public Use of the National Park System, 1872–2000* (Washington: Department of the Interior, National Park Service, U.S. Government Printing, Office, 1968), p. 87.

Favorite Ways to Explore Economics

1. The Park Service faces the problem of over-crowding. There are three basic solutions. Use shifts or other changes in the graphs provided below to demonstrate each of these three solutions.

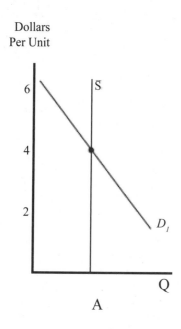

A

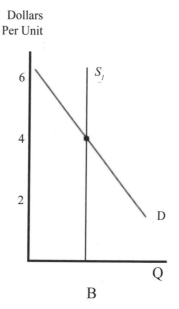

B

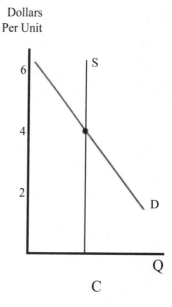

C

2. Which of the three solutions would you choose and why? (Be sure to list the advantage of your solution and the disadvantages of the others.)

3. Defend the statement that congestion is sometimes economically desirable.

4. Demonstrate the effect of letting hungry carnivorous grizzly bears roam free near the camping spaces in the park on the graph provided below.

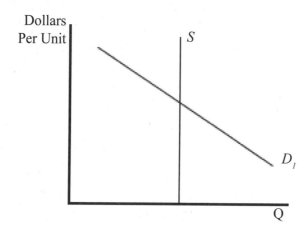

5. Demonstrate the effect of increasing the speed limit to 80 mph and simultaneously lowering the price of an annual park entry permit to $25.00 on the graph provided below.

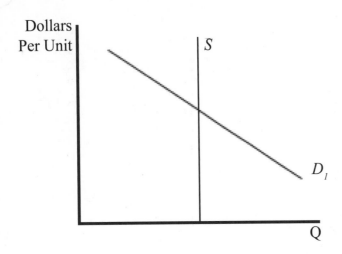

6. If the demand for park camping spaces tends to be inelastic, comment on the effectiveness of raising the price as a solution to overcrowding. How would your answer change if the demand for park camping were elastic?

7. Do you think the demand is inelastic or elastic? Why?

8. Do you agree or disagree that sometimes factors other than economics must be considered in cases like this?

Chapter 7
MACROECONOMIC INDICATORS, DEFICITS, AND DEBT
....

Classroom Experiment 7.A

COLAs and Living Burger-to-Burger on Route 66

Time Required: *10 - 15 minutes*	***Materials***: *none*	***Level of Difficulty:*** *low to moderate*
Purpose: *to provide experience with cost of living adjustments and insight into the world of price variations.*	***Textbook Coverage of Underlying Topics***: *Explorations in Economics:* Chapter 14	

INTRODUCTION

Entering the DeLorean in the movie *Back to the Future* would take you to a different time, when a hamburger at the same diner might cost a dime or $5, depending on the settings in the time machine. Entering a Chevy Volt in reality and driving in any direction can generate the same results. A hamburger costs about a dime in Tijuana, Mexico, and over $8 in the Hard Rock Café in New York City. Although acquiring the Chevy is up to you, in this experiment you will take a virtual tour to explore the cost of living across the country, and contemplate the reasons for variations in the price of a hamburger.

SCENARIO

You and your class will take the Internet highway down old Route 66 from Chicago to Santa Monica, with a few side trips along the way. Your instructor will assign you one city on the route, and you are to estimate the cost of a hamburger there, starting with the fact that a burger costs a dollar in Amarillo, Texas. If you use a salary comparison website like http://www.homefair.com/calc/salcalc.html, simply say that your salary is $100,000 in Amarillo, and ask it to tell you the equivalent amount in your assigned city. Divide by 100,000 to find the price of a burger. Alternatively, if you use cost-of-living index values for this calculation, you can apply the formula:

$$\frac{\text{Index Value for Your City}}{\text{Index Value for Amarillo}} \times 100 = \text{Price of Burger in Your City.}$$

After pricing burgers in your assigned city, try to find the highest and lowest prices in the USA. Perform your research prior to class, and fill in the following:

Your assigned city: _____

The price of a burger in your assigned city: _____

The most expensive city you could find (burger price and location): _____

The cheapest city you could find (burger price and location): _____

REFLECTIONS
(Please answer these questions *after* completing the classroom experiment.)

1. Why do prices change over time?

2. Why do prices differ in different places?

3. What prevents arbitrage between these cities? (Arbitrage is the process of buying at a low price and selling at a high price to gain riskless profit from unequal prices.)

4. Do the cross-country hamburger prices you came up with represent nominal or real values?

5. What would happen to the purchasing power of the money in your pocket if you moved from your assigned city to Amarillo?

AFTERTHOUGHTS

Variations in the cost of living across locations make some places a real deal and other places money pits. Supply and demand drive the cost of living, and popular places tend to generate high demand for goods and correspondingly high prices. If you happen to like places that aren't so popular, you can live relatively high on the hog. For example, radio disc jockey Rick Dees owns hundreds of acres and a private golf course in central Kentucky. If he stayed in Los Angeles where his radio show is produced, the same investment in real estate would hardly buy him a putt-putt golf course.

Classroom Experiment 7.B

Budgetary Woes: A Balancing Act

Time Required: *30 - 45 minutes*	***Materials:*** *none*	***Level of Difficulty:*** *moderate*
Purpose: *to provide insight into the challenges of budget allocation at the national level.*	***Textbook Coverage of Underlying Topics:*** *Explorations in Economics:* Chapter 15	

INTRODUCTION

The primary purpose of this exercise is to introduce the general categories of government expenditure and the difficulty of allocating funds among these categories. There are 311 million Americans, 535 members of Congress, thousands of lobbyists, and an infinite number of ways to allocate the federal budget. All of this spells trouble when it comes time for the budget to balance. You will be working with only three of your fellow students and the budget provided below has only 30 items. See how you do. You may find that your class could run government far more efficiently than the folks at it today, or you may gain an appreciation for the difficult economic dilemmas facing our representatives in Washington, D.C.

SCENARIO

You have $2 trillion that you and three other members of your government will allocate among the categories below. Typical expenditures and percentages are provided, first for spending on purchases and transfers, and then for "tax expenditures" on various tax breaks. You may well want to change these allocations of the budget. Just as members of Congress have personal and political reasons to favor certain areas, you will have your own priorities. In addition to your pre-existing preferences, suppose that you represent constituents with particular interests in several of these areas of spending. Notice that most of the spending categories below are labeled with a capital letter. The four people in your group, in alphabetical order according to your last names, have special interests in budget items A–F, G–M, N–S, and T–Z respectively. Upon reporting your group's results, you will receive a coveted invisible star and a silent clap for each 1 percent increase in spending on any of your special interests (as a percentage of the typical spending on those items), and you will lose one invisible star and silent clap for each 1 percent increase in spending on the special interests of your opponents. For example, suppose that one of your special interests is International Affairs and a special interest of someone else in the group is Transportation. If you agree on a budget that increases spending on International Affairs by 10 percent from 20 to 22, and increases spending on Transportation by 5 percent from 40 to 42, you get $10 - 5 = 5$ invisible stars. The percentage change is found using the formula:

$$\frac{\text{New Expenditure - Typical Expenditure}}{\text{Typical Expenditure}} \times 100$$

Before or at the beginning of class (depending on your instructor's assignment), come up with your personal budget plan. In class you will be assigned to a group of four with whom to try to hash out an agreement on the budget. Although some of the recent U.S. leaders have overindulged, you are not permitted to spend more than you have. If you come to an agreement, write up your master plan and you will have the opportunity to post it or present it to the class.

SPENDING	TYPICAL PERCENT	TYPICAL EXPENDITURE (IN BILLIONS)	YOUR PLANNED DOLLARS (IN BILLIONS)
A. Military Spending	13.65	273	_____
B. Veterans and Military Retirement	3.35	67	_____
C. International Affairs (aid, State Department, etc.)	1	20	_____
D. General Science, Space, and Technology	0.9	18	_____
E. Non-Defense Energy Spending	0.25	5	_____
F. Natural Resources and Environment	1.1	22	_____
G. Agriculture	0.75	15	_____
H. Commerce and Housing Credit	–0.55	–11*	_____
I. Transportation	2	40	_____
J. Community and Regional Development	0.7	14	_____
K. Education, Training, Employment, and Social Services	2.85	57	_____
L. Non-Medicare Health Spending	5.8	116	_____
M. Medicare	7.9	158	_____
N. Non-Social Security Retirement and Unemployment	3.35	67	_____

Favorite Ways to Explore Economics

SPENDING	TYPICAL PERCENT	TYPICAL EXPENDITURE (IN BILLIONS)	YOUR PLANNED DOLLARS (IN BILLIONS)
O. Social Welfare Spending (housing assistance, nutrition programs, home energy assistance, etc.)	5.65	113	_____
P. Social Security	16.85	337	_____
Q. Administration of Justice (FBI, border enforcement, law enforcement, civil and criminal prosecution, etc.)	0.95	19	_____
R. General Government Administration (tax collection, legislative functions, general property and records management)	0.75	15	_____
Net Interest Payments	11.8	236	_____
Undistributed Offsetting Receipts (contributions to retirement programs, rents and royalties on continental shelf, etc.)	−2.05	−41	_____
S. Corporate Tax Breaks	3.3	66	_____
T. Personal Business and Investment Benefits (capital gains, accelerated depreciation, other tax breaks)	3.65	73	_____
U. Pension and Retirement Plan Deductions	3.7	74	_____
V. Employer-Paid Health Insurance	2.7	54	_____
W. Itemized Deductions (mortgage interest, charitable contributions, medical expenses, state & local taxes, etc.)	4.15	83	_____
X. Earned Income Tax Credit	1.1	22	_____
Y. Untaxed Social Security Benefits	1.15	23	_____
Capital Gains on Homes	1.05	21	_____

SPENDING	TYPICAL PERCENT	TYPICAL EXPENDITURE (IN BILLIONS)	YOUR PLANNED DOLLARS
Z. Medicare-related tax deductions	0.65	13	_____
Other Personal Tax Expenditures (fringe benefits, workers comp, child care credits, soldiers andveterans, etc.)	1.55	31	_____
Total	100	2000	_____

*Housing credits are offset by receipts from loan guarantee programs.

REFLECTIONS

(Please answer these questions *after* completing the classroom experiment.)

1. If you came to an agreement, what was the secret to your success? If you didn't, what were the major impediments?

2. How did your budget differ from the real thing? Would the changes you proposed go over well in Congress?

3. What surprised you the most about the typical budget?

4. In what significant ways do you think resources would be allocated differently if budgets were designed in the absence of pork-barrel politics?

AFTERTHOUGHTS

There's an old saying that the two things one wouldn't want to see in the works are sausage and politics. Hopefully your negotiations weren't as ugly as the real thing, which has been known to shut down the government and occupy legislators for extended periods. For more practice at budget allocation, check out the excellent national budget simulation at http://www.econedlink.org/national-budget-simulator.php.

Problem Set 7.1

The Consumer Price Index

The only things the citizens of Econville eat are root beer and chips. These two goods do not change in quality over time and are produced in the same way each year. Econville citizens consume these in a 3 cases of root beer per 2 bags of chips ratio. The prices of these two goods are listed below. Assume that each year consumers purchase 3 cases of root beer and 2 bags of chips.

	ROOT BEER	CHIPS
2009	$6.00	$1.00
2010	$6.50	$1.25
2011	$6.75	$1.40
2012	$7.15	$1.50

1. Calculate the total cost of what the typical consumer purchases in Econville in each of the years listed.

2. Using 2010 as the base year, calculate the consumer price index for each year.

3. Use the consumer price index figures from question 2 to calculate the rate of inflation from 2009 to 2010, 2010 to 2011, and 2011 to 2012.

Problem Set 7.2

Inflation

If inflation is anticipated to be 5% per year and actual inflation for that year turns out to be 7%, identify whether each of the following groups would be helped or hurt by this, or if the effect is indeterminate, and why.

1. People who are living on fixed incomes.

2. Banks that have made long-term loans at fixed interest rates.

3. People who have purchased bonds.

4. A person who has purchased real estate with a bank loan.

5. A recent college graduate with many loans to pay back.

6. People who have purchased stock.

7. Governments that have sold bonds.

8. Savers with open passbook accounts.

9. People who have purchased precious metals.

10. Wage earners who are members of a strong union.

Favorite Ways to Explore Economics

Problem Set 7.3

Benchmarking Inflation

The following inflation figures were calculated using the Consumer Price Index for All Items (CPI-U), and represent the percent change from the previous year.

1960	1.7	1970	5.7	1980	13.5	1990	5.4	2000	3.4
1961	1.0	1971	4.4	1981	10.3	1991	4.2	2001	2.8
1962	1.0	1972	3.2	1982	6.2	1992	3.0	2002	1.6
1963	1.3	1973	6.2	1983	3.2	1993	3.0	2003	2.3
1964	1.3	1974	11.0	1984	4.3	1994	2.6	2004	2.7
1965	1.6	1975	9.1	1985	3.6	1995	2.8	2005	3.4
1966	2.9	1976	5.8	1986	1.9	1996	3.0	2006	3.2
1967	3.1	1977	6.5	1987	3.6	1997	2.3	2007	2.8
1968	4.2	1978	7.6	1988	4.1	1998	1.6	2008	3.8
1969	5.5	1979	11.3	1989	4.8	1999	2.2	2009	-.04

1. Plot the inflation rate for each year in the 1960s on the graph to the right. Calculate the average rate of inflation for that decade and draw a horizontal line on your graph at that rate.

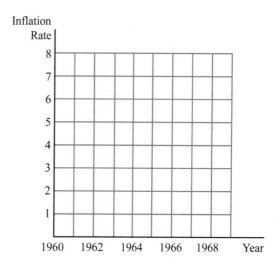

2. Plot the inflation rate for each year in the 1970s on the graph to the right. Calculate the average rate of inflation for that decade and draw a horizontal line on your graph at that rate.

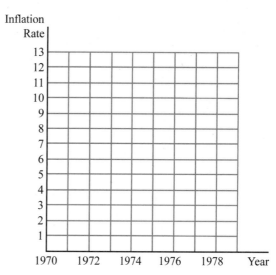

3. Plot the inflation rate for each year in the 1980s on the graph to the right. Calculate the average rate of inflation for that decade and draw a horizontal line on your graph at that rate.

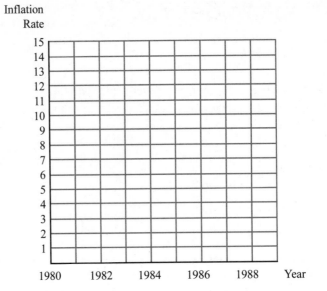

4. Plot the inflation rate for each year in the 1990s on the graph to the right. Calculate the average rate of inflation for that decade and draw a horizontal line on your graph at that rate.

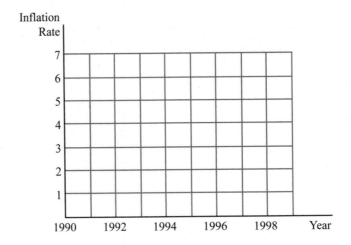

5. You guessed it! Plot the inflation rate for each year from 2000 through 2009 on the graph to the right. Calculate the average rate of inflation for that decade and draw a horizontal line on your graph at that rate.

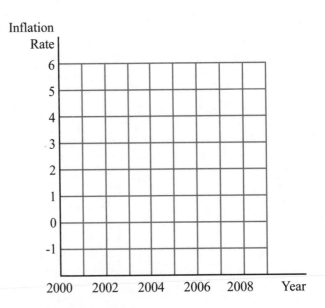

Favorite Ways to Explore Economics

6. An average inflation rate for a period in the past indicates what people living in that period—perhaps your parents or grandparents—were used to. Summarize your work for questions 1 through 5 by listing the average inflation rate for each decade studied.

7. What was the average inflation rate over the period from 1960 through 2009?

8. Do a bit of research to find the annual percentage change in CPI-U since 2009 and create your own graph like the ones above for the years from 2010 to the present.

Problem Set 7.4

Gross Domestic Product

The following figures are available for an economy:

Consumer expenditures = $600
Business expenditures = $150
Government expenditures = $200
Imports = $75
Exports = $65
Transfer payments = $50
Depreciation = $25

1. Calculate gross domestic product for this economy.

2. The GDP figure that you calculated above is for year 1 and is comprised of:

> 90 economics textbooks @ $10 each, and
> 40 economics workbooks @ $1 each.

> In year 2 this same economy produced:

> 90 economics textbooks @ $15 each, and
> 40 economics workbooks @ $2 each.

> Calculate nominal GDP for year 1 and year 2.

3. The value of the *GDP deflator* price index can be found for year 2 by dividing the nominal GDP in year 2 by the nominal GDP in the *base year* (year 1) and multiplying the result by 100. Calculate the year 2 GDP deflator for this economy.

4. The real GDP in a particular year can be found by dividing the nominal GDP in that year by the GDP deflator and multiplying the result by 100. Calculate the real GDP for year 2 for this economy.

5. Calculate the real GDP for a period when the nominal GDP is $1000 and the GDP deflator is 200.

Favorite Ways to Explore Economics

Problem Set 7.5

Economic Growth

The following growth rates represent the percentage change in real gross domestic product since the previous year. These figures come from the *Economic Report of the President*.*

1960	2.5	1970	0.2	1980	–.3	1990	1.9	2000	4.1
1961	2.3	1971	3.4	1981	2.5	1991	–.2	2001	1.1
1962	6.1	1972	5.3	1982	–1.9	1992	3.4	2002	1.8
1963	4.4	1973	5.8	1983	4.5	1993	2.9	2003	2.5
1964	5.8	1974	–.6	1984	7.2	1994	4.1	2004	3.6
1965	6.4	1975	–.2	1985	4.1	1995	2.5	2005	3.1
1966	6.5	1976	5.4	1986	3.5	1996	3.7	2006	2.7
1967	2.5	1977	4.6	1987	3.2	1997	4.5	2007	1.9
1968	4.8	1978	5.6	1988	4.1	1998	4.4	2008	.0
1969	3.1	1979	3.1	1989	3.6	1999	4.8	2009	–2.6

*preliminary data

1. Plot the growth rate for each year in the 1960s on the graph to the right. Calculate the average growth rate for that decade and draw a horizontal line on your graph at that rate.

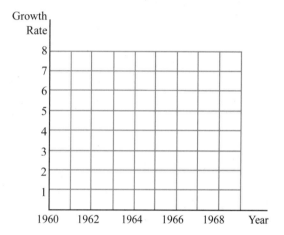

2. Plot the growth rate for each year in the 1970s on the graph to the right. Calculate the average growth rate for that decade and draw a horizontal line on your graph at that rate.

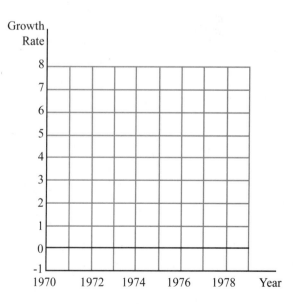

3. Plot the growth rate for each year in the 1980s on the graph to the right. Calculate the average growth rate for that decade and draw a horizontal line on your graph at that rate.

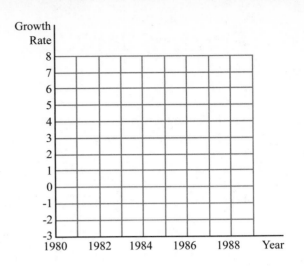

4. Plot the growth rate for each year in the 1990s on the graph to the right. Calculate the average growth rate for that decade and draw a horizontal line on your graph at that rate.

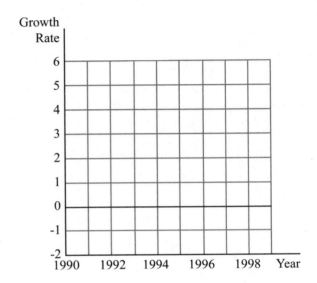

5. Plot the growth rate for each year from 2000 through 2009 on the graph to the right. Calculate the average growth rate for that decade and draw a horizontal line on your graph at that rate.

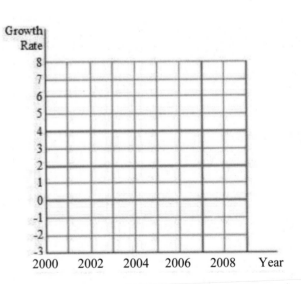

Favorite Ways to Explore Economics

6. Summarize your answers to questions 1 through 5 by listing the average rate of real GDP growth for each decade.

7. What was the average rate of economic growth over the period from 1960 to 2009?

8. Find data on the percentage change in real GDP since 2009 online and create your own graph like the ones above for the period from 2010 to the present.

Problem Set 7.6

Calculating the Unemployment Rate

The following formulas will be useful in answering the questions in this problem set:

Labor force = number of employed + number of unemployed

$$\text{Unemployment rate} = \frac{\text{Number of unemployed}}{\text{Labor force}} \times 100 \ \text{percent}$$

$$\text{Labor-force participation rate} = \frac{\text{Labor force}}{\text{Adult population}} \times 100 \ \text{percent}$$

Adult population	223 million
Employed	139 million
Unemployed	8 million
Not in labor force	76 million

1. Calculate the size of the labor force.

2. Calculate the unemployment rate.

3. Calculate the labor-force participation rate.

Problem Set 7.7

Types of Unemployment

Classify each of the following into the appropriate category of unemployment. Your choices are:

Frictional unemployment
Cyclical unemployment
Structural unemployment
Seasonal unemployment

1. An unemployed auto assembly line worker during a sales slump.

2. A snow plow driver during the summer.

3. A record player repairman who has not learned to fix digital music players.

4. A computer programmer who quits his job to look for a job with better benefits.

5. A high school dropout with few skills who has been looking for a job unsuccessfully for weeks.

6. A recent business school graduate looking for her first job.

7. A person whose job has been automated out of existence.

8. A vendor who sells hot dogs at major league baseball games, during the winter months.

9. A welder who finds that robots have replaced most of the welding jobs on assembly lines.

10. A top salesman for a computer company who quit because he did not like his boss.

Problem Set 7.8

The Natural Rate of Unemployment

The following unemployment rates represent the percentage of the labor force that is unemployed. The figures come from the *Economic Report of the President.*

1960 5.5	1970 4.9	1980 7.1	1990 5.6	2000 4.0
1961 6.7	1971 5.9	1981 7.6	1991 6.8	2001 4.7
1962 5.5	1972 5.6	1982 9.7	1992 7.5	2002 5.8
1963 5.7	1973 4.9	1983 9.6	1993 6.9	2003 6.0
1964 5.2	1974 5.6	1984 7.5	1994 6.1	2004 5.5
1965 4.5	1975 8.5	1985 7.2	1995 5.6	2005 5.1
1966 3.8	1976 7.7	1986 7.0	1996 5.4	2006 4.6
1967 3.8	1977 7.1	1987 6.2	1997 4.9	2007 4.6
1968 3.6	1978 6.1	1988 5.5	1998 4.5	2008 5.8
1969 3.5	1979 5.8	1989 5.3	1999 4.2	2009 9.3

1. Plot the unemployment rate for each year in the 1960s on the graph to the right. Calculate the average unemployment rate for that decade and draw a horizontal line on your graph at that rate.

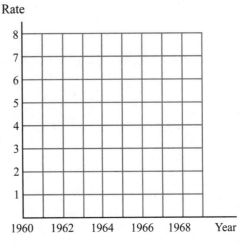

2. Plot the unemployment rate for each year in the 1970s on the graph to the right. Calculate the average unemployment rate for that decade and draw a horizontal line on your graph at that rate.

Favorite Ways to Explore Economics

3. Plot the unemployment rate for each year in the 1980s on the graph to the right. Calculate the average unemployment rate for that decade and draw a horizontal line on your graph at that rate.

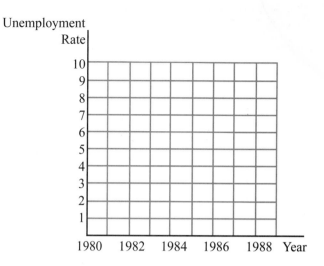

4. Plot the unemployment rate for each year in the 1990s on the graph to the right. Calculate the average unemployment rate for that decade and draw a horizontal line on your graph at that rate.

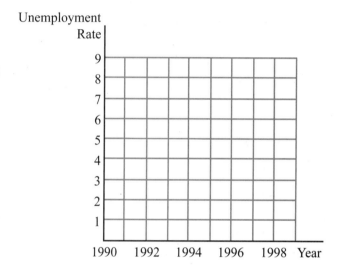

5. Plot the unemployment rate for each year from 2000 through 2009 on the graph to the right. Calculate the average unemployment rate for that decade and draw a horizontal line on your graph at that rate..

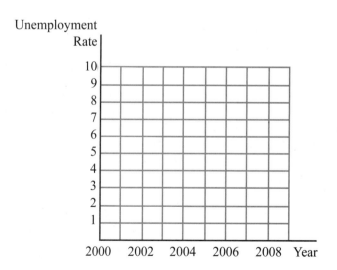

6. Summarize your answers to questions 1 through 6 by listing the average rate of unemployment for each decade.

7. What was the average rate of unemployment over the period from 1960 to 2009?

8. Locate unemployment figures online and create your own graph like the ones above for the years from 2010 to the present.

Favorite Ways to Explore Economics

Problem Set 7.9

Real vs. Nominal Values

The following are box office receipts for the some of the highest grossing movies of all time as listed on www.movieweb.com. These values are in millions of actual (nominal) dollars, meaning that no adjustments have been made for inflation.

TOP ALL TIME HIGHEST GROSSING MOVIES
(Gross domestic ticket receipts in $ millions)

ALL TIME RANKING	RECEIPTS	TITLE	YEAR OF RELEASE
1.	$759	Avatar	2010
2.	$601	Titanic	1997
3.	$533	The Dark Knight	2008
4.	$461	Star Wars: Episode IV – A New Hope	1977
5.	$437	Shrek 2	2004
6.	$435	E.T.	1982
7.	$431	Star Wars: Episode I – The Phantom Menace	1999
8.	$423	Pirates of the Caribbean: Dead Man's Chest	2006
9.	$415	Toy Story 3	2010
10.	$408	Spider-Man	2002
11.	$402	Transformers: Revenge of the Fallen	2009
12.	$380	Star Wars: Episode III- Revenge of the Sith	2005
13.	$377	The Lord of the Rings: The Return of the King	2003
14.	$373	Spider-Man 2	2004
15.	$371	The Passion of the Christ	2004
16.	$357	Jurassic Park	1993
17.	$342	The Lord of the Rings: The Two Towers	2002
18.	$340	Finding Nemo	2003
32.	$309	Star Wars: Episode VI – Return of the Jedi	1983
44.	$290	Star Wars: Episode V – The Empire Strikes Back	1980
54.	$260	Jaws	1975
70.	$239	Ghostbusters	1984
76.	$233	The Exorcist	1973
111.	$199	Gone with the Wind	1939
124.	$185	Snow White and the Seven Dwarfs	1937
131.	$181	Grease	1978
181.	$160	The Sting	1973
182.	$159	The Sound of Music	1965
226.	$142	The Jungle Book	1967
434.	$103	Bambi	1942

The following are figures for the GDP deflator:

1937	13.5	1980	60.4	1990	93.6	2000	117.6
1939	13.7	1981	66.1	1991	97.3	2001	120.1
1942	15.0	1982	70.2	1992	100.0	2002	121.9
1965	25.0	1983	73.2	1993	102.6	2003	123.9
1967	27.8	1984	75.9	1994	105.0	2004	125.5
1970	30.6	1985	78.6	1995	107.6	2005	126.0
1973	35.4	1986	80.6	1996	109.7	2006	130.2
1975	42.2	1987	83.1	1997	111.9	2007	134.0
1977	47.5	1988	86.1	1998	114.8	2008	136.8
1978	47.5	1989	89.7	1999	114.9	2009	138.1
						2010	139.5

The real value of a movie's earnings can be estimated by dividing the nominal GDP in the year of the movie's release by the GDP deflator in that year and multiplying the result by 100.

1. Use the nominal figures from the movie list and the GDP deflators above to create a list of the top 5 highest grossing movies of all time in real dollars. Compare your results to the top five highest grossing movies in nominal dollars.

Chapter 8
MONETARY AND FISCAL POLICY

Classroom Experiment 8.A

Stock Market Games: Predicting the Effects of Policy and Animal Spirits

Time Required*: 20 minutes at the beginning and end of the several-week period of the game*	***Materials****: Internet access*	***Level of Difficulty:*** *low to moderate*
Purpose: *to provide engagement in financial economics and exposure to the workings of the stock market.*	***Textbook Coverage of Underlying Topics****:* *Explorations in Economics:* Chapters 15 and 17	

INTRODUCTION

Financial markets bring those who want to invest money and take on risk together with those who want to borrow money and reduce risk. The bond market and the stock market serve these purposes, as do financial intermediaries such as banks. Perhaps the most watched financial markets are stock markets. Stock prices respond to actual and anticipated monetary and fiscal policy. They also change due to optimism and pessimism, which economist John Maynard Keynes described as *animal spirits*. Investors like Warren Buffett have made fortunes by predicting market reactions to policies and changes in the economy. Many others have lost fortunes due to bad predictions. For that reason, the educational adventure of stock trading is extremely risky—unless you're just pretending. Virtual stock market games offer the education without the risk, and a growing number of websites provide good games at little or no charge.

SCENARIO

You or your instructor can choose from a variety of Internet stock market games. Examples include:

• The Virtual Stock Exchange (http://www.virtualstockexchange.com/), which promotes a variety of competitions based on pretend trading of real stocks.

• The Stock Market Game™ (http://www.smgww.org/), a program of the Securities Industry Foundation for Economic Education, an affiliate of the Securities Industry Association.

• The Hollywood Stock Exchange (http://www.hsx.com/), in which you buy and sell shares of celebrities and productions in a virtual exchange.

The Iowa Electronic Markets (http://tippie.uiowa.edu/iem/) offer real-money markets for outcomes of different types, including elections and Federal Reserve monetary policy. As an alternative to all of the above, your instructor may simply ask everyone in the class to pick $50,000 worth of stocks today, and then see whose stock portfolio increased in value by the largest percentage over a four week (+/-) period. There are also useful online descriptions of the myriad trading symbols and terms to complement this Internet activity. See, for example, Yahoo! Finance (http://finance.yahoo.com/), and the New York Stock Exchange Website (http://www.nyse.com).

REFLECTIONS
(Please answer these questions *after* completing the classroom experiment.)

1. In what way is the stock market valuable to corporations?

2. In what way is the stock market valuable to investors?

3. As an investor, you bore some of the financial risks faced by the corporations whose shares you held. How did those risks play out and how did you respond to those risks?

4. What strategy did you employ in your mock stock investing?

5. In an efficient market, the prices of the stocks should reflect all available information, meaning that opportunities for exceptional profit or loss occur only on a random basis. Why do you suppose some people consistently make large profits in the stock market, while others lose their shirts?

AFTERTHOUGHTS

Financial markets are central to the success of our economy because they bring cash-strapped entrepreneurs together with cash-laden investors, and risk takers together with those who want or need to avoid them. Futures markets serve a similar purpose, allowing farmers (for example) who can't afford the downside risk of price fluctuations to obtain a certain price for their unplanted crops by selling the rights to those forthcoming crops to speculators who think the price will go up. With humble beginnings such as Osaka's Dojima Rice Exchange in the 1730s, these markets are in many ways to thank for our current supply of food and commercial goods.

Problem Set 8.1

Fiscal Policy

1. Fill in the appropriate fiscal policy action in each square of the table, indicating the **direction** in which the policy tool above the square (government spending or taxation) should be changed to bring about the appropriate change in the problem to the left of the square (recession or inflation).

	Government Spending	Taxation
Recession		
Inflation		

Problem Set 8.2

Monetary Policy

1. Fill in the appropriate monetary policy action in each square of the table, indicating the **direction** in which the policy tool above the square (open market operations, reserve requirements, or the discount rate) should be changed to bring about the appropriate change in the problem to the left of the square (recession or inflation).

	Open Market Operations	Reserve Requirements	Discount Rate
Recession			
Inflation			

Problem Set 8.3

Fiscal Policy and Monetary Policy

The federal government uses fiscal policy to act in a counter-cyclical manner. The Federal Reserve uses monetary policy for the same reason. Indicate the specific policy solution that would address the problems below within the given guidelines.

1. Monetary policy to correct for inflation, using the discount rate.

2. Fiscal policy to correct for inflation, using government spending.

3. Monetary policy to correct for inflation, using the reserve requirement.

4. Fiscal policy to correct for inflation, using tax changes.

5. Monetary policy to correct for inflation, using open market operations.

6. Monetary policy to correct for recession, using the discount rate.

7. Fiscal policy to correct for recession, using government spending.

8. Monetary policy to correct for recession, using the reserve requirement.

9. Fiscal policy to correct for recession, using tax changes.

10. Monetary policy to correct for recession, using open market operations.

Chapter 9
MONEY AND BANKING

Classroom Experiment 9.A

Money Creation Experiment: Banks and Borrowers

Time Required: *20 - 30 minutes*	**Materials**: *100 pennies or funny-money dollars*	**Level of Difficulty:** *low to moderate*
Purpose: *to simulate the money-creation process and demystify this intricate reality.*	**Textbook Coverage of Underlying Topics**: *Explorations in Economics:* Chapter 17	

INTRODUCTION

Money doesn't grow on trees, but believe it or not, it can be created almost out of thin air by the banking system. The U.S. has what is called a fractional reserve banking system in which only a fraction of total deposits is held on reserve in the banks' vaults and the rest is lent out. The ratio of a bank's reserves to a bank's deposits is called its reserve ratio, and the Fed sets a minimum reserve ratio for all banks. Deposits beyond the required reserves are called excess reserves and may be lent out. Banks earn profits by lending out their deposits at an interest rate a few percentage points higher than the rate they pay their depositors. In this experiment you will be part of the money creation process and see how much money the banking system can "grow" out of a small initial deposit.

SCENARIO

As an individual, it isn't wise to hold much cash on hand because inflation erodes its value, not to mention the fact that it might get lost or stolen.

In this exercise we will make the simplifying assumptions that individuals hold all of their money in banks, and that banks loan out all of their excess reserves. Sitting in a semi-circle (if possible), every other person will be a banker and the others will be borrowers. In real life, people borrow money from banks to spend it, and the businesspersons who receive that money from the spenders are likely to deposit it into their own banks. This experiment best exhibits money creation if we have as many banks and borrowers as possible, so we will cut out the businessperson role and assume that the borrower deposits the money directly into a bank account. Of course, for realism, we can think of this as the bank account of the businessperson from whom something was purchased.

Your instructor will deposit a dollar into the first bank (the first person in the semi-circle) and announce the required reserve ratio. The first bank can then lend the excess reserves to the first borrower (the second person in the semi-circle). The first borrower deposits all of these funds into the second bank (the third person in the circle), and so the process goes until there is no more money or no more people.

Use the space below to record your holdings.

If you are a bank, indicate the amount of money you are holding as required reserves: _____

If you are a borrower, indicate the amount of money you have on deposit: _____

DEPOSIT (PENNIES)	REQUIRED RESERVES	LOAN
100	20	80
80	16	64
64	13	51
51	10	41
41	8	33
33	7	26
26	5	21
21	4	17
17	4	13
13	2	11
11	2	9
9	2	7
7	2	5
5	1	4
4	1	3
3	1	2
2	1	1
1	1	0
Total ≈ 500	Total = 100	Total ≈ 400

(Totals are approximate due to rounding.)

REFLECTIONS
(Please answer these questions *after* completing the classroom experiment.)

1. The required reserve ratio was _____. In the end, the total amount of money being held in banks was _____, and the total amount depositors had in their bank accounts was _____.

2. Economists claim that the money multiplier, equal to one divided by the required reserve ratio, tells us the total increase in the money supply created from each $1 in new deposits. Using the numbers from this experiment, check the veracity of the economists' assertion.

3. What would the total deposits have been after the money creation process in this experiment if the required reserve ratio had been 0.10? _____ How about if the required reserve ratio had been 0.50?

_____

4. What do you suppose would happen if the initial depositor decided to withdraw her $1?

AFTERTHOUGHTS

Your answers to question 3 indicate the sensitivity of the multiplier to the reserve requirement. In theory, modest changes in the required reserve ratio can result in large changes in the amount of money on deposit, and therefore change the money supply. Money creation is indeed an important phenomenon in our economy, although open market operations and adjustments in the discount rate turn out to be more viable tools for monetary policy. One reason for this is that banks seldom loan out all of their excess reserves, making changes in the required reserve ratio relatively ineffectual. If we ever pay off our national debt, the Treasury will no longer need to borrow money by selling bonds, and the Fed will no longer be able to buy and sell those bonds on the open market to influence the money supply. That possibility makes money creation and alternative methods of influencing the money supply important topics.

Classroom Experiment 9.B

Barter vs. Money: Appreciating the Dollar

Time Required*: 10 - 15 minutes*	***Materials****: a chair, a pen, an eraser, a piece of chalk, and a lectern*	***Level of Difficulty****: low*
Purpose: *to demonstrate some of the virtues of money.*	***Textbook Coverage of Underlying Topics****:* *Explorations in Economics:* Chapter 16	

INTRODUCTION

Money serves several valuable purposes in our economy. It provides a standard unit of account that makes price comparisons far easier than if backpacks cost 22 chickens at one location and 13 sacks of flour at another. It is a store of value that allows ski instructors to buy food in the summertime because they can convert their wintertime service into money that is readily storable until times of need. And it is a medium of exchange that frees us from having to barter for what we need. In a barter economy, those needing to purchase something hope for a *double coincidence of wants*, meaning that when two people get together to barter, each will want what the other has. Bartering is seldom facilitated by such luck. In this experiment you will see what happens when it is not.

SCENARIO

This experiment is inspired by an episode of the old Korean War situation comedy *M*A*S*H,* in which the surgical unit needs penicillin, but the people who have penicillin don't want anything that the surgical unit has. This precipitates a series of bartered trades of what the unit does have for what other parties have ultimately to gain the penicillin. In the classroom experiment, someone who only has a chair to trade will seek out a pen. With chair in hand, the pen seeker will visit with the people on his street (row of desks) one at a time, starting with those closest to him or her, trying to barter for a pen by obtaining that which the pen owner desires. He or she can ask the neighbors what they have and what they would be willing to accept for their possessions. (Items cannot be appropriated from any other source.) As you watch or participate in this experiment, you will gain first-hand understanding of the complexity of life without money.

REFLECTIONS
(Please answer these questions *after* completing the classroom experiment.)

1. How would this experiment have been different if everyone had $100 in cash?

2. How often does the person who has what you want, want what you have, creating a double coincidence of wants?

3. Beyond the lack of double coincidences of wants, what other problems are presented by the need to barter?

4. In what settings might bartering be necessary because money is unavailable?

5. Some people see money as the root of evil. Would things be better if we didn't have money?

AFTERTHOUGHTS

Money turns out to be a blessing, despite its reputation as a source of greed. The ease of exchange, value storage, and accounting using a standard form of money have led most civilizations to concoct some form of money, be it shells, arrowheads, carved stones or precious metals. Perhaps in most societies it was the refrigerator salesperson who was first to push for the adoption of a common currency. (Refrigerators are heck to carry around and barter with!)

Problem Set 9.1

Bank Expansion of Demand Deposits

In a fractional reserve banking system, an initial deposit in a bank can lead to a larger total bank expansion of the money supply. Assume that all banks can immediately loan out all of their excess reserves, that the reserve requirement is 20% of deposits, and that all excess reserves loaned out are deposited into another bank.

If a stranger comes into Econville and deposits $2,000.00 into Bank 1:

1. How much will Bank 1 have to keep in reserve?

2. How much will Bank 1 be able to loan out as excess reserves?

3. How much will be deposited into Bank 2?

4. How much will Bank 2 have to keep in reserve?

5. How much will Bank 2 be able to loan out as excess reserves?

6. How much will be deposited into Bank 3?

7. How much will Bank 3 have to keep in reserve?

8. How much will Bank 3 be able to loan out as excess reserves?

9. How much will be deposited into Bank 4?

10. How much will Bank 4 have to keep in reserve?

11. How much will Bank 4 be able to loan out as excess reserves?

12. How much will be deposited into Bank 5?

13. How much will Bank 5 have to keep in reserve?

14. How much will Bank 5 be able to loan out as excess reserves?

15. If this process continues what will eventually be the total expansion of the money supply?

16. How much of the money in question 15 was created by the banking system?

Problem Set 9.2

The Reserve Requirement and the Money Multiplier

The Central Bank sets the reserve requirement for the banking system of Econville. All banks in Econville must keep the required reserves on deposit at the Central Bank or in their vaults in the form of cash. All banks loan out their excess reserves.

A $10,000.00 deposit is made into a bank in Econville. For the following reserve requirements fill in the amount of required reserves.

1. 10%

2. 20%

3. 25%

4. 33 1/3 %

5. 50%

For each of the following reserve requirements fill in the amount of excess reserves.

6. 10%

7. 20%

8. 25%

9. 33 1/3%

10. 50%

The money multiplier is 1 divided by the reserve requirement. For each of the following reserve requirements fill in the money multiplier.

11. 10%

12. 20%

13. 25%

14. 33 1/3%

15. 50%

The total amount by which the money supply can expand is the money multiplier times the amount of the initial deposit. For each of the following reserve requirements fill in the amount by which the money supply could expand with an initial deposit of $10,000.

16. 10%

17. 20%

18. 25%

19. 33 1/3%

20. 50%

Problem Set 9.3

Money Market

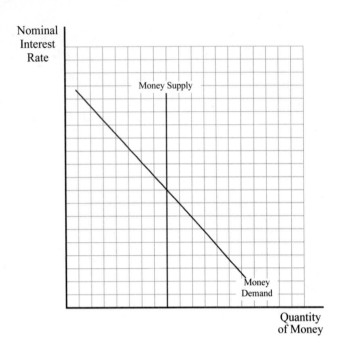

For each of the following actions indicate (a) what shift(s) would occur in the graph above and (b) the resulting change in the nominal interest rate.

1. The Federal Reserve sells bonds on the open market.

2. The Federal Reserve raises the reserve requirement.

3. The Federal Reserve lowers the discount rate.

4. The economy expands and people experience an increase in their income level.

5. The Federal Reserve buys bonds on the open market.

6. The economy enters a recession and people experience a decrease in their income level.

7. The Federal Reserve lowers the reserve requirement.

8. The Federal Reserve raises the discount rate.

9. The Federal Reserve sells bonds on the open market and at the same time the economy is contracting and people experience a decrease in their income level.

10. The Federal Reserve buys bonds on the open market and at the same time the economy is expanding and people experience an increase in their income level.

Chapter 10
AGGREGATE SUPPLY, AGGREGATE DEMAND, AND THE CIRCULAR FLOW

Classroom Experiment 10.A

Getting into the (Circular) Flow of Things

Time Required: *15 - 20 minutes*	**Materials:** *inhibition*	**Level of Difficulty:** *low to moderate*
Purpose: *to reinforce understanding of the circular flow.*	**Textbook Coverage of Underlying Topics:** *Explorations in Economics:* Chapter 2	

INTRODUCTION

What goes around comes around. This universal truth is central to macroeconomics as well. The factors of production—land, labor, capital, and entrepreneurship—flow from households to firms through the factor market, and then back to households in the form of goods and services via the product market. Dollars flow in the opposite direction, going from households to firms in exchange for goods and services via the product market, and then back to households in exchange for inputs via the factor market. We are all parts of this flow in one way or another. To follow the entire path within the course of a few minutes is to gain a fuller and more memorable perspective on the circular flow than most people are fortunate enough to experience.

SCENARIO

Okay, stop thinking about chocolate because you're about to be a refrigerator. That's right. You read over the circular flow description but it didn't soak in because you didn't pretend you were a refrigerator and ride the tide, so buck up and put on a chill. You and the rest of the class will tour the circular flow, taking the role of inputs, goods, or the money exchanged for them. To be more specific, you will represent the inputs that go into refrigerators, the refrigerators themselves, and then money on the return trip. Your instructor will designate the four corners of your room as households, factor markets, firms, and product markets respectively. Starting at home in the household corner, the class will shuffle through the factor markets to the firms as labor, steel, plastic, and coolant. The firms transform these inputs into refrigerators (representing all goods and services) and you will shuffle as a fridge from the firms through the product markets to the households. After arriving in a household kitchen you will change form and direction and head to the product markets as money. The expenditure on refrigerators in the product markets goes to the firms, where you take a right turn and the money goes to the factor market as payment for the inputs that went into production. Think about what you are as you move from one place to another. Once you've made it around in both directions, try it once more for good measure.

REFLECTIONS
(Please answer these questions *after* completing the classroom exercise.)

1. In what sense can we say that "what goes around comes around" in this context?

2. What are some of the complexities of the real-world circular flow that are left out of this simple model?

3. What would happen if there were a significant snag in one section of the circular flow? For example, what if an energy crisis prevented refrigerators from being delivered from the product markets to the households?

4. What does it mean when people say that "firms don't pay taxes, people do"?

AFTERTHOUGHTS

Are you dizzy? Thanks for going along for the ride. It's important to know how the various sectors of our economy fit together and feed into each other. When you're asked to recount the journey of the circular flow on the exam, it will be nice to know that you've been there and done that.

Problem Set 10.1

Aggregate Supply and Aggregate Demand

Use an aggregate supply and aggregate demand diagram like the one shown below to demonstrate the effect of each of the following changes. In each case make only one shift, in either aggregate supply or aggregate demand.

Example: The government decreases spending and increases taxes.

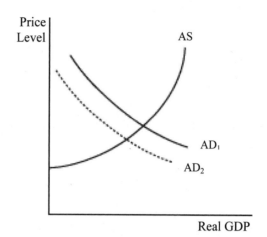

1. Consumer confidence grows for the third straight month.

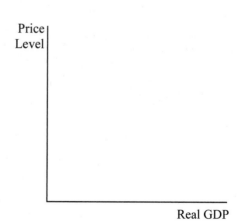

2. A technological breakthrough lowers the cost of energy.

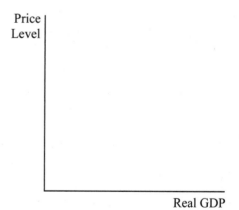

3. The government engages in a new highway construction program.

Price Level

Real GDP

4. A series of natural disasters disrupts the production and delivery of goods and causes a negative supply shock.

Price Level

Real GDP

5. Oil prices increase and a series of bad weather events destroy crops.

Price Level

Real GDP

6. Interest rates fall, causing an increase in consumer and business spending.

Price Level

Real GDP

Favorite Ways to Explore Economics

7. Labor productivity rises and costs fall throughout the economy.

Price Level

Real GDP

8. A war destroys capital and disrupts production.

Price Level

Real GDP

9. Increased graduation rates for schools lead to a more-skilled workforce resulting in a positive supply shock.

Price Level

Real GDP

10. Stock and bond markets soar, which results in higher household income levels.

Price Level

Real GDP

Chapter 11
INTERNATIONAL ECONOMICS
••

Classroom Experiment 11.A

The Benefits from Trade: Utility Gains from a Lunch Sack

Time Required: *10 - 15 minutes*	***Materials***: *Each person needs one or more random knick-knack worth about 25 cents (lunch sack optional).*	***Level of Difficulty:*** *low*
Purpose: *to demonstrate the gains from trade*	***Textbook Coverage of Underlying Topics***: *Explorations in Economics:* Chapter 18	

INTRODUCTION

Our global community struggles with issues of international trade and how open it should be, but certain aspects of trade should be clear. This experiment illuminates the potential benefits of trade. Iraq has oil, the U.S. has fields of wheat, and Columbia produces excellent coffee. The act of bringing these varied goods to the trading table provides opportunities for increased satisfaction for every country involved. Mutually beneficial trades draw on our comparative advantages and cater to our differing preferences. In this experiment we feel those benefits first-hand.

SCENARIO

Your instructor will either supply or ask you to bring in one or more knick-knacks, "white elephants," or other tradable items. You will have the opportunity to conduct trades with classmates during a five-minute trading period. First, let's gauge your degree of happiness.

Given your current state of affairs and possessions, including the knick-knack you obtained for this experiment, how happy are you on a scale of 1 to 100? A rating of one means that you are utterly and completely unhappy, a rating of 50 means that you are feeling so-so, and a rating of 100 means that you are in eternal bliss. What's your number? _____

Your classroom is your microcosm of the world. When the trading period begins, take your tradable item(s) around the classroom and see if you can make one or more trades to acquire items that you prefer over your own.

REFLECTIONS
(Please complete these *after* the trading period has ended.)

1. On a scale of 1 to 100, how happy are you now that the trading period is over?.

2. When your instructor surveyed the class to see how many were happier after trading than before, roughly what proportion of your class reported that they were happier?

3. Why is it unlikely that anyone was made worse off as the result of the trading period?

4. Explain how an improvement in the overall happiness level of your class was achieved without bringing any additional resources into the classroom.

5. What implications do these findings have on the advisability of trade? What drawbacks from trade must be considered when formulating trade policy?

AFTERTHOUGHTS

My elementary school had no cafeteria. I would bring a sack lunch each day and spend the first five minutes of the lunch period trading what I had for what others had. My house had an abundance of canned fruit and Halloween candy, whereas my friends had sandwiches that I wasn't good at making and other foods not available in my home. It was not difficult to find mutually beneficial trades. The experiment above, like lunchroom food bartering, provides a simple-yet-striking example of the gains from trade. The message is not that free trade is always good, but that we must not neglect its potential to make things better for everyone involved.

Classroom Experiment 11.B

Comparative Advantage Experiment: To Everyone's Advantage

Time Required: *20 - 30 minutes*	***Materials***: *none*	***Level of Difficulty:*** *moderate. Players are asked to negotiate terms of trade, which isn't always easy.*
Purpose: *to provide first-hand knowledge of the conditions under which mutually advantageous trade is possible, and to reinforce understanding of the concepts of comparative and absolute advantage.*	***Textbook Coverage of Underlying Topics***: *Explorations in Economics:* Chapter 18	

INTRODUCTION

There is heated disagreement among policymakers regarding the opportunity to benefit from trade. Protectionists worry that poorer countries can't provide real benefits to richer countries, and that for a rich country to trade with a poor country is tantamount to giving the poor country charity money. Advocates of free trade argue that two countries can benefit from trade as long as the relative costs of producing goods differ between the countries.

Economists say a country has a **comparative advantage** over another country in the production of a good if, in order to make each unit of the good, it foregoes less in terms of the production of other goods than the other country. In other words, it has a lower "opportunity cost" of producing the good. A country has an **absolute advantage** over another country in the production of a good if it can make that good using fewer inputs per unit of output than the other country. If the two countries have identical resources and both countries devote their resources to the production of the same good, the country with the absolute advantage would be able to produce more of the good than the country with the absolute disadvantage.

SCENARIO

Consider yourself a dictator in charge of trade for a country. (Your instructor will tell you which country you represent and with which country you are trading.) The graphs below represent the production possibilities for each of the countries. For example, using all of its resources, in one period (let's call it a day), country A could produce 40 cars if it devoted all of its resources to car production, 40 computers if it devoted all of its resources to computers, or any of the combinations of cars and computers represented by points on the production possibilities frontier. It cannot make both 40 cars and 40 computers, for example, because each point on the line is only possible using *all* of the country's resources. As you learned in the links and smiles experiment, or will learn soon enough in your class, it is a simplification to have these lines straight rather than curved.

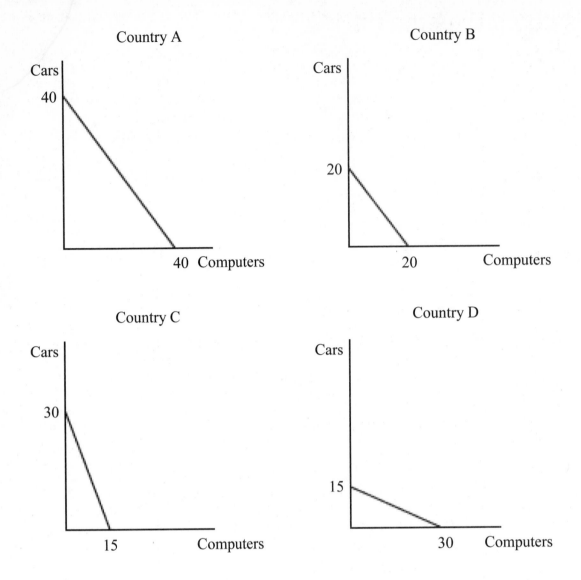

Country A

Cars
40

40 Computers

Country B

Cars
20

20 Computers

Country C

Cars
30

15 Computers

Country D

Cars
15

30 Computers

Assume that in the absence of trade, your country chooses to make exactly half of its maximum capacity of both goods. That is, the midpoint on the production possibilities frontier is the most favorable point for you. You are to negotiate with the representative of the country you are paired with to see if you can establish terms of trade—an exchange of some quantity of goods that you produce for some quantity of goods that the other country produces—that provide both countries with more of both goods than without trade. If you come to an agreement, write down the number of cars per computer in your exchange, and the total number of cars and computers that changed hands. You will have 10 minutes to complete this negotiation. There are three questions you should consider before you begin your negotiations:

1. What is your opportunity cost for making each car? _____

2. What is your opportunity cost for making each computer? _____

3. What is the range of trade prices, in cars per computer, that would benefit your country **and** the country you are negotiating with?

(Hint: Calculate each country's opportunity cost of computers. If trade should occur, it is wise for each country to export what it has a comparative advantage in, and import what it has a comparative disadvantage in. The mutually beneficial range of trade prices [in cars per computer] are those that exceed the opportunity cost of computers for the computer-exporting country, and fall below the opportunity cost of computers for the computer-importing country.)

REFLECTIONS

(Please answer these questions *after* completing the classroom experiment.)

Which country did you represent? _____

Which country did you negotiate with? _____

Between your country and the country you were negotiating with:

1. Which had a comparative advantage in cars? _____

2. Which had a comparative advantage in computers? _____

3. Which had an absolute advantage in cars? _____

4. Which had an absolute advantage in computers? _____

5. Explain the trade agreement, if any, that you made with the representative you were paired with, and why both parties were willing to participate in this trade.

6. Beyond international trade, list two other situations in which comparative advantages might lead to benefits from specialization and exchange.

7. On the graph below, draw the production possibilities frontier for your country. Indicate with an "X" the point that represents the number of cars and computers that your country will *produce* after trade. Then indicate with a big dot the point that represents the number of cars and computers that your country can *consume* per period after your trade.

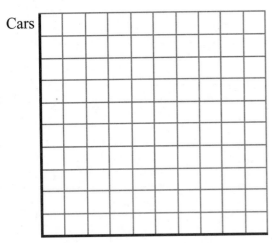

Cars

Computers

8. Are there any two countries that would not be able to form a mutually beneficial trade agreement? Explain.

AFTERTHOUGHTS

Now you can probably guess where economists generally stand on the debate over free trade. Impediments to free trade such as tariffs, quotas, and other protectionist policies prevent the mutual gains available whenever one country has a comparative advantage over another. If you're thinking it's time to get more economists in Congress, we're with you!

Problem Set 11.1

Exchange Rates

Currency markets establish the international value of a nation's monetary unit. The exchange rate determined in these markets is a function of the supply of, and the demand for, these various currencies. The following table lists fictional exchange rates for selected countries.

	EXCHANGE RATE
France (euro)	.80 equals U.S. $1.00
Canada (dollar)	1.40 equals U.S. $1.00
Japan (yen)	150.00 equals U.S. $1.00
Britain (pound)	50 equals U.S. $1.00

Using the values in the table above, calculate the following:

1. A $150.00 hotel room in the U.S. would cost a Japanese tourist _____ yen.

2. A $30,000.00 American car would cost a Canadian citizen _____ Canadian dollars.

3. A $15.00 compact disk from the U.S. would cost a person from France _____ euros.

4. A $5,000.00 Canadian dollar fly-in fishing trip would cost an American _____ U.S. dollars.

5. A $2,000.00 weekend at Disneyworld in Orlando, Florida would cost someone from England _____ British pounds.

Answer the following questions using the assumption that the values in Table 1 have changed to those shown in Table 2.

EXCHANGE RATE

France (euro)   0.80 equals U.S. $2.00
Canada (dollar)   1.40 equals U.S. $2.00
Japan (yen)   150.00 equals U.S. $2.00
Britain (pound)   .50 equals U.S. $2.00

6. American-made goods would become relatively _____ to citizens of other countries.

7. Foreign-made goods in America would become relatively _____.

8. The price of domestically made goods in America would _____.

9. American exports would _____.

10. American imports would _____.

11. The U.S. dollar has _____ from the values shown in Table 1 to those shown in Table 2.

Problem Set 11.2

Comparative and Absolute Advantage

The countries of Karenville and Laurenland are able to produce root beer and pretzels. The following figures represent the output that can be produced with a fixed amount of factor inputs.

	KARENVILLE	LAURENLAND
Root beer	10	12
Pretzels	20	30

Answer the following questions on the basis of the information above.

1. Which country has an absolute advantage in the production of root beer? Explain how you arrived at your answer.

2. Which country has an absolute advantage in the production of pretzels? Explain how you arrived at your answer.

3. Which country has a comparative advantage in the production of root beer? Explain how you arrived at your answer.

4. Which country has a comparative advantage in the production of pretzels? Explain how you arrived at your answer.